ETHNOMUSICOLOGY

A study of Intercultural Musicology

S.A.K. Durga
Director
Center for Ethnomusicology
Madras
and
Professor Emeritus
Department of Indian Music
Madras University

B.R. RHYTHMS
Delhi - 110052

Published by:

B.R. Rhythms
425, Nimri Colony, Ashok Vihar, Phase-IV
Delhi-110 052
E-Mail : *brpc@vsnl.com*

2017

2004 *Revised and enlarged edition*

ISBN 9788188827015

Printed at Balaji Offset, Delhi

Cataloging in Publication Data--DK
Courtesy: D.K. Agencies (P) Ltd. <docinfo@dkagencies.com>

Durga, S. A. K., author.
Ethnomusicology : a study of intercultural musicology / S.A.K. Durga.
pages cm
Includes bibliographical references.
ISBN 9788188827015

1. Ethnomusicology. 2. Music--Asia--Foreign influences. I. Title.

ML3798.D87 2017 DDC 780.89 23

This work is dedicated to my parents Smt. & Sri. S.A. Venkataraman not only because of the special nature of such a kinship relation, but because it is they who led me into the very special world of music.

CONTENTS

CONTENTS

FOREWORD

The theoretical principles of ethnomusicology (designed by Westerners) largely reflect Western interests and priorities and are of dubious value for non-western societies. If Western ethnomusicologists were truly interested in the "preservation" and development of the music cultures of non-western societies, they would design theories that would lead, for example, to greater creativity in non-western idioms of music and to more jobs and income for non-western composers, performers and scholars. Instead, the theories of ethnomusicology, as they currently exist, are designed to provide job security for Western academics. Even so, these theories have had only short term effectiveness, judging by the increasingly fewer jobs available to Western ethnomusicologists in Western institutions.

The theoretical principles of ethnomusicology are mostly based on information derived from the analysis of non-western music cultures and it is therefore paradoxical that the views of non-western scholars are little reflected in the discipline. The status quo suggests that ethnomusicology is a western rather than global discipline and in order to give it a global status, Westerners need to recognize that their non-western colleagues have their own perceptions of the discipline and that these perceptions should be given a voice.

There is indeed a need for non-Western ethnomusicologists to find their own voice, for although they have become increasingly active in the discipline, they have tended to practise it as defined by Westerners, subduing their own voice in the process. This position is unlikely to continue much longer, however, and it is my view that non-western scholars will become influential in the actual definition of the field.

This book by Dr. Durga is a process in the right direction, an effort to empower other non-western scholars by giving voice to her own perceptions.

The concept of intercultural musicology, which Dr. Durga articulates in this work, is to my mind a major breakthrough and her foresight in introducing the concept into the literature is commendable. In my definition, intercultural musicology is (a) the study of one's own indigenous music culture using techniques that are applicable to other music cultures or (b) the study of music cultures other than one's indigenous culture, irrespective of the techniques used in such a study. Intercultural musicology includes those areas of scholarship that belong to ethnomusicology but also accommodates aspects of modern interculturalism (for example, symphonic music based on elements of non-western traditional music) which seem to lie outside the scope of ethnomusicology. The concept of intercultural musicology encourages a healthy attitude towards change and innovation in music.

Dr. Durga's book is not only a valuable model for non-western scholarship in music but also one that Western ethnomusicologists cannot afford to ignore. The non-western voice can only become more and more decisive and the trend manifested by Dr. Durga's book is unlikely to be reversible.

Akin Euba
University of Pittsburgh, USA

PREFACE

The new discipline Ethnomusicology is widely known throughout the world but the term "Ethnomusicology" has become an unsatisfactory terminology for many musicologists and Ethnomusicologists in India and other countries especially in non-western countries because of the prefix "Ethno" before musicology. The term Ethnomusicology was introduced by Jaap Kunst, a Dutch Ethnomusicologist in 1950 who was dissatisfied with the term 'Comparative Musicology'. Through the years, Ethnomusicology like any other academic field began to widen its scope through research and teaching of the subject at the various universities in the world. After five decades, the prefix "Ethno" before Musicology lost its meaning, purpose and context for which it was attached with the term Musicology for this discipline. The study of world musics with socio-cultural perspective has made the discipline Ethnomusicology more as a study of Intercultural Musicology.

My Doctoral study in Ethnomusicology at Wesleyan University, Connecticut, USA and my Post-Post Doctoral Research at the Yale University, USA in Ethnomusicology and my teaching experience at the S.N.D.T. Women's University, Bombay, India as visiting Professor where I teach the Course "World Musics" from 1987 gave me an insight to understand that the discipline Ethnomusicology is a study of Intercultural Musicology.

The present work deals with the concept of Intercultural musicology, the emergence of Ethnomusicology in India from late 19th Century by British writers and the Intercultural aspects in the classical musics of India and the musical and theatrical traditions of South East Asia and South Asia to emphasise that Ethnomusicology is a study of Intercultural musicology.

I express my sincere thanks to Prof. John Blacking for his invaluable suggestions and inspiring discussions which helped me to understand the concept of Intercultural Music/Musicology during his visit to India and to my center for Ethnomusicology at Madras in 1987 and Dr. Akin Euba, Director, Centre for Intercultural Music Arts, London and Andrew Mellon Professor, Department of Music, University of Pittsburgh USA for his encouragement to work on this area and also for his kind acceptance to write the Foreword for my work.

INTRODUCTION

Ethnomusicology is a branch of Musicology which gives special emphasis for the socio-cultural perpective to the study of World Music Cultures. This phenomenon has transformed the discipline Ethnomusicology into Intercultural Musicology. "The relationship among most of the world's cultures has become so close that cultural interaction viewed through music has become a major focus of Ethnomusicological research" (Nettl: 1986).

The term Ethnomusicology was first coined by Jaap Kunst in 1950 to replace the term 'Comparative Musicology'. The discipline began to grow through the years and the definitions for the term Ethnomusicology began to change according to the modifications of its concept such as "Musicology" Systematic musicology", "Cultural Musicology" and "Intercultural Musicology". The prefix "Ethno" before Musicology has lost its meaning, purpose and context for which it was attached. Ethnomusicology is "the study of *any* and *all* Musics" (Hood : 1972) became an acceptable definition.

Ethnomusicology was also viewed as the study of music outside one's own culture and the discipline was introduced as "World Musics" program in many American Universities instead of "Ethnomusicology". The nature of Ethnomusicological studies has been enlarged during the past fifty years and at the fag end of the 20th century, Ethnomusicology has turned into a study of intercultural Musicology mainly because of its methodology - the socio-cultural perspective on the world Musics cultures. In 1972 Gilbert chase remarked "I favour the idea of Ethnomusicology... but I do not favor the terminology ... What we need is a term of lager scope ... For this I propose the term "Cultural Musicology" (220p). Though the term "Cultural Musicology" was preferred to identify Ethnomusicology, the socio-cultural perspective on Music brought forth the various types of inter-cultural relationships or acculturation that have taken place in the history of World Music Cultures. Ethomusicology is oriented more towards Intercultural studies and is a study of Intercultural Musicology.

Prof. Bruno Nettl is of the opinion that "if there is any official date for the beginning of inter cultural studies in Ethnomusicology, it is 1952 the year of the publication of Richard Waterman's work about Syncretism" (1991:558p.)

It can be said that when the discipline Ethnomusicology began to focus on the study of other music cultures from one's own and followed the methodology to study the musics with socio-cultural perspective, the intercultural aspects in all Musics in the World are revealed. Therefore it will be more appropriate to describe Ethnomusicology as a study of Intercultural Musicology than cultural musicology.

"Ethnomusicology is an approach to the study of any Music not only in terms of itself but also in *relation to the cultural contexts*" (Hood; 1978) also points out that the discipline Ethnomusicology is oriented towards the study of Cultural Musicology.

The present work describes the differences between Musicology and Ethnomusicology by bringing out the methodological variations, and the growth of the discipline for the past five decades which has brought forth number of definitions by practitioners for the term Ethnomusicology. The present day focus of Ethnomusicology on the Intercultural Music studies reveal that All Musics are Intercultural in the sense that the Intercultural Aspects in Music are found in Religious, Traditional, classical, Folk and popular musics of the world. This work studies as to how the intercultural aspects in the scholastic tradition of Indian music has brought forth the Emergence of Ethnomusicology in India. Intercultural aspects in the performing tradition of the classical Musics of India, the "Hindustani" system of North India, the "Sufyana Kalam", the Classical Music of Kashmir and the "Karnatic" system of the South India; and the western influence upon the Asian Musics and Intercultural aspects in the Musical and Theatrical traditions of South East Asia and South Asia are also dealt with in detail.

The first chapter entitled "Understanding Ethnomusicology" describes the birth of the new discipline and its growth through the years, the second chapter "Ethnomusicology as a Methodology" discusses the various methodologies used in the study of Ethnomusicology, the third chapter "Ethnomusicology and Folk Music Research" describes the scientific methodologies to be used for the study of Folk Music with special reference to Indian Folk Music and the importance of Documentation, Field work and Field Techniques in the Folk music research as emphasised in Ethnomusicology. The fourth chapter "Ethnomusicology in India" brings out the contributions of British writers on Indian Music and the beginning of intercultural Musicology with the English writings on Indian Musicology.

From the fifth chapter onwards the intercultural Music studies in Ethnomusicology are brought out through a study on the Intercultural aspects in the Musics of Asia. The fifth chapter deals with western influence upon the Musics of Japan, China, India and Indonesia. The sixth chapter speaks about the Intercultural aspects in the performing Traditions of Indian Classical Musics - the North Indian "Hindustani" system, the classical Music of Kashmir - the "Sufyana Kalam" and the South Indian "Larnatic" system. The seventh chapter is on the Indian Influence upon the Musical and the Theatrical Traditions of South East Asia with special reference to Ramayana Theatre of India and South East Asia. The last chapter brings out the Intercultural aspects in the Non-Classical Musics of South Asia" - Bangladesh, India, Nepal, Srilanka and Pakistan.

The purpose of the present work is to highlight the concept of Intercultural studies in Ethnomusicology to emphasise that Ethnomusicology is more a study of Intercultural Musicology.

CHAPTER I

UNDERSTANDING ETHNOMUSICOLOGY

Ethnomusicology is a branch of Musicology. This discipline developed after World War II in Western countries with a special emphasis on the inter-disciplinary approach to music. Like any other academic field which is being created and recreated through research, writing and teaching of its practitioners, Ethnomusicology also had many variations in concepts, interpretations and applications.

The discipline Ethnomusicoloy branched out of Musicology because of the ardent desire of many Western musicologists to study non-western musics which exist with oral traditions and especially with the tribal and village communities of the non-western countries. The term Ethnomusicology was introduced by Jaap Kunst, a Dutch Musicologist in 1950, though the discipline was in existence in the name of comparative musicology from late 19th Cent. It may be said that from the publication of the Viennese Scholar Guido Adler, "UMFANG METHODE UND ZID DER MUSIKWISSENSCHAFT" (1885) the term comparative Musicology was used for the study of non-western musics as a separate branch of musicology. The first edition of Harvard Dictionary defines Comparative Musicology as the 'study of exotic music' as "the musical cultures outside the European Tradition" (Willi Apel: 167p and 205p 1944).

After World War II, the term comparative musicology was not faoured by many musicologists and one of them was Jaap Kunst, the Dutch Ethnomusicologist who argued that "the term (comparative musicology) is not entirely satisfactory however for the comparative method is frequently used in the other fields of musicology and studies in this field are often not directly comparative". Therefore Jaap Kunst introduced the term Ethnomusicology in his little booklet MUSICOLOGICA in the title page of the book (7p) in 1950. He placed the prefix "Ethno" in front of the Word Musicology with a Hyphen to indicate that the study would be on the music of the races of man or Ethnic group.

The term was virtually accepted immediately and a Society fo Ethnomusicology was established in 1956 at the United States of America. The general consensus of the members who framed the society discussed and favoured the view that "Ethnomusicology is by no means limited to the so called "primitive music" and is defined more by the orientation of the student than by any rigid boundaries of discourse ---. The term Ethnomusicology is more accurate and descriptive of this discipline and its field of investigation than the older term comparative musicology. (1956, 5p). The hyphen in Ethnomusicology was officially dropped by the Society for Ethnomusicology in 1957. Prof. David Mcallester, one of the the founders of the Society for Ethnomusicology emphasised that this new discipline must not be defined by Music under study but by its methodology.

By the second half of the decade of 1950s the term Ethnomusicology came into use with or without hyphen as synonyms and by the end of the decade, the term comparative musicology reached a status of a historic term.

The term Ethnomusicology has been defined by many Ethnomusicologists from time to time changing the connotations of the terms. Jaap Kunst defined the term Ethnomusicology as the study of "Mainly the music and musical instruments of all non-European peoples, including both the so called primitive peoples and the civilised Eastern Nations" (7p, 1950). In the Third Edition of this same book, he wrote that a study of "Traditional Music and Musical Instruments of All cultural strata of mankind but specifically named "Tribal and Folk Music" and every kind of non-western Art Music" specifically excluding Western Art and popular Music (p.1, 1959). This definition was satisfactory at that period for many Ethnomusicologists. More definitions for the term Ethnomusicology began to come up from 1960s from various Ethnomusicologists extending the scope of study wider and wider.

The definitions of noted Ethnomusicologists are the following

Ethnomusicology is "the study of music "in" and "as" culture (Merriam: 1968). The definition of Geroge List stressed the importance of oral tradition. "Ethnomusicology is to a great extent concerned with music transmitted by unwritten tradition" (1962, 24p).

Geroge List remarked in 1979 that "The field of study known as Ethnomusicology has expanded so rapidly that it now encompasses almost any type of human activity that conceivably can be related in some manner to what may be termed music. The data and methods used are derived from many disciplines found in the Arts, the Humanities, the Social Sciences and the Physical Sciences. The variety of philosophies approaches and methods utilised is enormous. It is impossible to encompass them all within one definition" (1979 1p).

Prof. Bruno Nettl defined the term as "a study of music outside one's own society and culture" (1969) Prof. Mantle Hood remarked that "Ethnomusicology is an approach to the study of any music, not only in terms of itself but also in relation to the cultural contexts (1969). The definition given by Prof. Mantle Hood was acceptable to many Ethnomusicologists though modifications on the definition are keep coming up todate.

It may be summed up that Ethnomusicology is a branch of musicology and this discipline obtains its individual character by its emphasis for the inter-disciplinary methodology to Musicology.

Charies Seeger in his foreward to Prof. Mantle Hood's work "The Ethnomusicologist" remarks "Ultimately there would be no roles for separate studies Musicology and Ethnomusicology but there would still be a distinction between the Musicological and Ethnomusicological approaches, the first to the thing in itself, he second to the thing in its cultural context as one of quite a number of other contexts." (1982, V-VI).

From 1970s, the discipline Ethnomusicology meant the study of World Musics and the Ethnomusicological approach or method began to be defined as the study of music in cultural Anthropological, Sociological and Musical perspectives. Prof. John Blacking remarked that "Ethnomusicology is a comparatively new word which is widely used to refer to the sduty of the different musical styles of the world" (1974) bringing out the present day concept of the term Ethnomusicology as the study of World Musics.

As Ethnomusicology emphasises the socio-cultural approach to music from 1960s, the terminology 'cultural musicology' was suggested for Ethnomusicology. (Chase:

1972) Prof. David Mcallester in his article "The Astonished Muse" remarks that "some of the underlying assumptions we started within the Society (SEM) and in the discipline of Ethnomusicology have changed and we are confronted with a different world in 1978 from that of 20 years ago when Ethnomuse was a fledging in Pinefeathers" and "what we have been calling Musicology and Ethnomusicology" might better be called "Mix Musicology" the term would remind us that the process of music making is the process of change and the assimilation of new ideas" (Journal of the Society for Ethnomusicology, May, 1979, 182p.) Ethnomusicological studies on western classical music also have come from 1980s (Wachsmann, 1981, 1982 and Marcia Herndon, 1988) and the term does not mean the study of non-western musics alone in modern days.

At the fag end of the 20th Century the connotation of Ethnomusicology has become widened and is understood as a scientific study of all the process and products of Music making in different cultural contexts.

Prof. Akin Euba, is the first non-Western Ethnomusicologist to suggest an alternate term for Ethnomusicology as "Intercultural Musicology' at a Round Table conference at the University of Pittsburgh, USA in 1995. He defines the term intercultural musicology as

1. "The study of one's own indigenous music culture using techniques that are applicable to other music cultures or

2. The study of music cultures other than one's own indigenous culture irrespective of the techniques used in such a study. Intercultural Musicology includes those areas of scholarship that belong to ethnomusicology but also accomadates aspects of

modern interculturalism (for example, symphonic music based on elements of non-western traditional music) Which seem to lie outside the scope of ethnomusicology. The concept of intercultural musicology encourages a healthy attitude towards change and innovation in music".

It may be said that by 21st Century, the term "Ethnomusicology" can be replaced by the more appropriate terminology, "Intercultural Musicology", because of its approach, methods and range of the subject matter.

Ethnomusicology emphasises "objective" methods and follows the western methodological developments of the late 19th Century which are known as scientific methods. Depending on the scholar's orientation, the methodology of Ethnomusicology is focussed on anthropoloical, social, cultural and musical perspectives. After 1980s the concepts of anthropology and musicology were fused and the interest was shown more to the processes of musical creation and performances - composition and improvisation - and the focus was to make critical examination than to collect information. New methodological tools are used to analyse the music and of its cultural setting which include aspects of cybernetics, information theory, semeiotics and structuralism. The style and structure of music is studied in detail for which the methodological tools the Transcription and analysis are used. Transcription is a subjective interpretation of a sounding musical phenomenon and its transformation coded into a graphic form which may be described as a graphic statisation of a dynamic sound form. Thus Transcription simultaneously analyses the music material. The method of transcription simultaneously analyses the music material. The method of transcription depends largely upon the purpose of transcription. It acts as a device for solving analytical problems and therefore the selection of the type of transcription must be the right one to help one's specific investigating problems such as comparison of sectional length in an extended improvision, types of ornaments used by the performers and composers, identification of rhythm and total variations and other musical characteristics. The analysis makes the process complete for the scientific investigation of the music material. The tools which are used for investigating musical factors are the measuring instruments for pitch intervals and duration, Notation Melograph, Audio Video Machines, and Movie Cameras of high quality and personal computers. All these tools help the analytical research to be more accurate and precise. The methodology is also oriented towards the cultural, social and anthropological perspectives which influence the music, the product and the producers. The study of music is made as Music "in" and "as" culture. The contextual technique which is normally used in the analysis of Linguistic and Ethnographic data emphasises the study of music in culture which is principally a perceptive approach requiring both analysis and synthesis.

Music as an event occurring in various contexts, the Ethnomusicologist analyses such events and the components of the context of the immediate situation as observed by studying.

1. Participants
2. Relevant actions
3. Relevant musical instruments
4. Music in terms of tonal and textual analysis.

The general context of culture is also analysed by examining

1. Different occasions of performance and the values in terms of which they take place
2. The relationship of musical events with other aspects of culture
3. Factors which affect the musical practice through acculturation or inter-cultural influence
4. Tradition and change in music culture and intercultural influence in music cultures are studied with historical perspectives.

Prof J.H. Kwabena Nketia remarks that "Ethnomusicology is deeply committed to Field work, for it is the primary tenet of the discipline that music must be observed and studied as an event, even where such music exist in the form of scores, so that statements can be made about various aspects of performance, the context of the performance and their relationship to music, the participants and the sequence of activities of phases of the occasion", (1985 : 115p.)

The important hallmark of Ethnomusicological research is the concept of field work with its many ramifications. Music in culture is studied either as a Microcosm of the culture in the sense that the musical culture replicates in detail the total cultural and social system that people have adopted or the music is considered as a commentary of that particular culture existing somehow outside the culture itself and reaching to what goes on in the society either by reflecting it or even by denouncing it through exhibiting opposite characteristics and tendencies.

Historical research is made by Ethnomusicologists who are interested in the processes through which music changes. The extrapolation of historical strata from a repertory presently extant has been a characteristic of historical Ethnomusicological research, Research is made on the history of individual compositions as they have unfolded into their many different versions with their cultural contexts. The Ethnomusicologists observe the processes as they occur to assess them and to find out whether from one particular set of evolving cultural conditions to predict certain types of musical changes and the ways in which various types of intercultural relationships or acculturation takes place. Ethnomusicology is mainly concerned with the present phenomenon of world Music culture - Westernization, Innovation Modernization and Urbanization and all types of cultural interactions subsumed under the general term Intercultural Music. Ethnomusicologist is specially interested in what has happened in world musics history at large by taking a broad view of the concept of change and tries to understand what types o changes happen under various circumstances and conditions in which cultures find themselves in the modern period and particularly in the ways in which various types of intercultural activities happen in world music.

The study of music as a socio-cultural phenomenon has led scholars to look at musical events in relation to performers and other participants in Music and more especially at the musicians social and economic status in the society. Problems of meanings, values and the norms of musical style as well as the mechanisms for ensuring continuity of tradition or for controlling stability and change and historical pocesses in different musical traditions have been the areas of interest for Ethnomusicologists.

Thus Ethnomusicologists strives for an "All embracing approach" that deals with any music and "everything that can shed light on the human context' of music. Ethnomusicology encompasses the study of Folk Music, Art Music Religious Music, Contemporary Music of World Music cultures, musical change, music as symbol, Universals in Music, the function of music in society, the comparison of musical systems, and study of other musical cultures from their own in musicological and cultural perspectives which distinguish Ethnomusicology from Musicology and has emerged as Intercultural Musicology.

CHAPTER II

ETHNOMUSICOLOGY AS A METHODOLOGY

The discipline Ethnomusicology which is the study of World Musics and intercultural musicology is also described as a perspective or methodology in the sense that music is studied in the socio-cultural perspective besides the application of scientific methodology using transcription and analysis to study the music.

Analysis helps the musicologist to study the style of music, folk or classical in a systematic way in order to be precise in describing musical process instead of using-general and subjective terms such as "beautiful" or "touches one's heart". A socio cultural perspective in musical study helps to understand the concepts of earlier writers by looking into the society and culture to perceive the reasons for changes in musical style and the intercultural aspects.

The term methodology has been defined as "the science of method or orderly arrangement specifically the branch of logic concerned with the application of the principles of reasoning to scientific and philosophical inquiry" (weber's, 1979, 927p). A methodology comprises of

1. Sources of Data and

2. Treatment of Data

Precepts of the scientific method tendeing towards logical and objective ways of thinking were first initiated and used by researchers in the natural sciences and have been applied to research in almost all disciplines, including music since the late nineteenth century. The western methodological developments of the late nineteenth century is known as scientific method. The scientific method which is the experimental approach to the subject is considered as being the most appropriate method to be used for music also to arrive at objective observations.

The field of Ethnomusicology which developed after world war II began to adapt western scientific method as its goal is to be "objective". First, ethnomusicology began as a study of the music of other cultures and secondly it attempted to compare the music cross-culturally to detect the intercultural concepts and universal patterns in music.

In order to study the othet music culture, the field work becomes very important for the ethnomusicologist. By undertaking field work, the ethnomusicologist not only collects the date for research but also tries to understand the culture of the other society and gets the first hand information of the music and people. The ethnomusicologist uses the sophisticated audio-visual tools for documenting the information. Besides collecting data, the ethnomusicologist tries to learn the music of the other culture under a teacher during the field trip and becomes reasonably proficient in performing the music.

The analysis of the music is made by transcribing the music. The western staff notation is used widely and sometimes additional symbols are introduced by the researcher to write down the music more accurately. The electro-acoustical devices such as the oscillograph, sonograph melograph and also personal computers are resorted to study the music objectively.

The transcription acts as a device for solving analytical problems and the ethnomusicologist selects the type of transcription to help the specific investigating problem such as comparison of section length in an extended improvision, types of ornaments used by the performers during the performance of a specific recital, identification of rhythm and total variations in the performance. Though many procedures for analysis have been devised, two types of systems are commonly in use. One attempts to provide a framework for all musical phenomena of the world or for all imaginable kinds of music and to make it possible within this framework to describe and compare musics. The other comprises of approaches that are culture-specific, derived in each case from the music under study and if possible, based on the theoretical system developed by the culture that has produced the music. Prof. Bruno Nettl states that there are many approaches that fall between these extremes and one of the unfortunate characteristics of Ethnomusicology is that there has been no standardisation of analytical procedures Ethnomusicologists are interested in music as a phenomenon produced by the culture and how the music changes with the period of time through the years. The problems are approached with a mixture of simple and complex methods (1972).

The methodology is based on the problem and also on the researcher's orientation. Musicologically trained researchers' concern is the style and structure of the music for which the methodological tools - transcription and analysis - are used. Anthropologically trained researches are interested in studying the socio-cultural developments or social changes of the period in which the musical style undergoes changes and therefore the methodology of Cultural Anthropology is used. The study of music is made as "in" and "as" culture (Merriam

1960) instead of separating music as an individual component unrelated to the performer or composer.

The contextual technique, which is normally used in the analysis of linguistic and ethnographic data, stressed the study of music in culture by Ethnomusicologists which is principally a perceptive approach requiring both analysis and synthesis.

Ethnomusicology began as a kind of offspring of musiology and Anthropology. Therefore musicologically oriented Ethnomusicologists learn to perform the other style of music in which the research study has to be done and write down the music in notation and transcription for analysis. Structural and stylistic analysis are made through transcriptions which vary from one individual to another depending upon the purpose of their transcription for solving specific analytical problem. Sometimes, their methodology is adopted from linguistics and French anthropological structuralism.

Anthropologically oriented Ethnomusicologist are interested in music as a phenomenon produced by a culture. They try to encapsulate entire cultures or establish a framework for comparative study or attempt to show correlations between musical types and cultural types and single out the cultural determinants of music to point out that certain types of culture produce certain types of music.

Historical methods are used by Ethnomusicologists who are interested in the process through which music changes. The extrapolation of historical strata from a repertory presently extant has been a characteristic of historical Ethnomusicological research. Research is made on the history of musical forms or on an individual composition as it unfolds into many different versions. Researches also pursue interests in the conventional study of the history of musical characteristics.

In this case, the Ethnomusicologists attempt to observe processes as they occur to assess them and to find out whether from one particular set of evolving cultural conditions they will be able to predict certain types of musical changes and the ways in which various types of inter cultural relationships affect musical styles.

The term "scientific" is often understood to be synonymous with "precise", "correct", "valid" and "true". The conception of science is naive because it perpetuates the myth that every conclusion which the modern 'scientific' method produces is true in an absolute sense. A scientific method is one which makes statements which are consistent with the postulates of a particular logical system. The criterion of validity for a scientific method is its measure of logical consistency. There is great pressure in this age of technology to be scientific, that is to analyze things logically.

But these logical systems can provide only *Relative Truth* and not Universal Truth. The relativity of logical truth means that an absolute objectivity cannot be established.

Prof. Bruno Nettl writes that "In 1880s, the Ethnomusicology began with a group of scholars saying "the rest of the musical world is just too different from western music" and thus need a discipline or sub-discipline of its own. A set of methods and approaches had to be developed that had not been used by the traditional music scholars, the historians of Art Music. And so field work, Transcriptions Comparative analysis, bimusically ethnographic interpretation, reflexivity and much more were brought to bear on this need to deal with what was different about non-western and folk music cultures" (1989: 72p). Ethnomusicologist in other words looked only for a "Scientific" methodology to be objective and not to present value Judgements on musical facts.

Ethnomusicology focusses on the study of music as a socio-cultural phenomenon which has led scholars to look at musical events in relation to performers and other participants in music. Problems of meaning, values and the norms of a musical style as well as the mechanisms for ensuring continuity of tradition or for controlling stability and change and historical processes in different musical traditions have engaged the attention of scholars.

It may be said that Ethnomusicologists are striving for "an all-embracing approach" that deals with any music - whether cultivated as an oral or written tradition and the processes related to music making in different socio cultural context, as well as "everything that can shed light on the himan context" of music. When the Ethnomusicologist deals with music as culture, the studies are made on the a) Ethnography of music b) The role and function of music in terms of the inter-relations of music and other aspects of culture and c) the cultural history of music Prof. Nketia remarks that the methodology of Ethnomusicology attempts or should attempt to integrate the objectivity of empirical observation and rational systamatisation with experience of the culture being studied for although music is a phenomenon whose constituents can be systmatised, it is also dynamic and involves processes that can be perceived or experienced aesthetically and socially". (1982: 640p).

"If then, there is a methodology in the field of ethnomusicology, it must, revolve around these five characteristics of the field. The interest in universals balanced by appreciation of infinite variety, the emphasis on field work, the possibility of notating and analysing music visually and verbally, the insistence that music can be understood only in its cultural context, and the interest in processes. This configuration of approaches seems to me to constitute the essence of ethnomusicology" (Nettl: 1980, 7-8p).

Ethnomusicology, the discipline which has developed as an independent science opted the scientific methodology of the late nineteenth century to be objective. The utopian aim to be objective ends up with statements of inter subjective nature. In any musicological research, the pure objectivity cannot be achieved and only the subjective experiences will be postulated objectively through scientific method.

Scientific truths are relative to the particular paradigms in which they are a part. Social theorists such as Jurgen and Habermas are urging that the effects of the scientific ideology which pervades western culture be re-examined. In the West throughout the nineteenth century, the scientific developmental notion of progress became a key concern in the realm of both the natural and the newly created social sciences research. This period marked a critical turning point in music research.

Warren Dwight Allen remarks that "from the enlightenment onward, music historians began to reject the notion of celestial music and to devote themselves to measurable, comparable, and knowable musical entities" (1962). The invention of the phonograph in the latter quarter of the nineteenth century helped to capture the scale and pitch - the ingredients of musics - on records and they were then measured and examined according to the procedures of science. But how far these scientific truths help the music world is a big issue. some extremists wonder if it helps at all. Does the scientific method of analysing music separate it from its musical quality? Many musicologist question whether music considered as "sound" in experiments in the laboratory brings out the facts about sounds but not about music. Though the question, "What is music? stands unanswered music is definitely not sound alone.

The scientific method - the formulation of hypotheses, the collection of data, the control of variables and finally, the formulation of generalisation about music behaviour - is believed to be the methodology of Ethnomusicologists and western musicologists of the twentieth century. On one very important level, this methodology itself elevates testable "data" over that which is not so easily subject to quantifiable analysis. In other words, in the face of demands of the scientific design, the Ethnomusicologist tends to elevate musicial sound over music behaviour. The former fulfills the scientific characteristics of "data" which can be captured and preserved by the portable recorder, while the latter is far more elusive, unpredictable, and almost impossible to capture on the recording machine. With the gravitation toward "hard data" the field phase may be subsidiary to the laboratory phase. Since the Ethnomusicologist many times is not able to converse and communicate through the language of the people under study, there may be a barrier in understanding the reality of their culture and music.

As it is ultimately the Ethnomusicologist who performs these scientific tasks, he is an indispensable part of the research process itself, a "variable" to be accounted for. Compounding the distorting effects of the scientific procedure itself is this subject object orientation of the observer who may assume his own objectivity and infallibility. In studying the music of other cultures, the Ethnomusicologists sometimes disclaims performance except as a mini methodological device.

The gathering of musical data is by means of sound recordings. The methods used to make recording affect the results. It is important to consider the performance situation which may be classified as (1) Performances which are performed in the normal course of events (2) those which are arranged for the purpose of recording and (3) interview performances where the researcher assumes a measure of control in selecting music, text, playing techniques, and whatever is essential for his study by demonstration and discussion. The nature of the performance situation undoubtedly has a bearing upon the data, and recordings are to some extend subjective documents as the choice is made by the researcher, mostly, and also depends upon the availability of the subject.

The limitations of notation and transcription are often discussed but still they form the main methodological tools. A complete piece of music is a memory and sensory onstruction of an organized sound phenomenon which may be noted or transcribed by theorists for study. The method of transcription depends largely upon the purpose of transcription. The transcriptions are affected by the perceptions. The use of western staff notation for inappropriate styles of music is another factor which may affect the transcription. Different systems of notation emphasise different aspects of the musical phenomenon : A transcription done at a lower speed that the actual performance cannot be said to be the right source for analysis. One needs to comment upon a music actually heard and not dissected.

Facts and value judgements are sometimes confused. In the scientific method, facts are tested and examined and observations are reported as accurate. This may be true depending upon the 'facts' considered for verification and the tools chosen to examine the facts. In some cases, value judgements are argued as facts. The rules of logical deduction and rules for arriving at true consequences derive from true premises. Induction is the process of reasoning from a part to a whole and from particulars to generals. The fact is tested deductively, but the observations determine its validity. Since it is impossible for the scientist to observe all possible situations, the scientist generalises from what is thought to be true of some observations. The represents a problem of induction and any empirical science begins with particular observation and subsequent generalisation. The controls one uses in the process of answering questions increase the likelihood of the answers being acceptable and functional.

Scientific method does not establish absolute truth, but it does help one to sharpen knowledge and understanding of the facts in evaluating theories. In the field of music, the subject is the human product, "music" for which human engage their ears and mechanical tools to verify their observations. Judgements made by human as to "objectivity" of their statements are always questionable.

Observations in music are always "inter-subjective" - subjective experiences are postulated objectively at many points in stylistic analysis of performers and composers.

Nazir. A. Jairazbhoy in his article. "The Objective and subjective View in Music Transcription" discusses in detail the limitations of transcriptions made by methanical devices like the melograph and points out "that we can never hear the 'objective' sound of the automatic transcriber" and that "all our music has been structured on the basis of what we hear, the subjective and distorted rather than the 'objective'. He further states that the mechanical transcription can never be a replacement for aural transcription and that "aural transcription by a trained Ethnomusicologist who has steeped himself in that culture may well be far more meaningful" (1977 : 263-270p). Thus, even the modern technologies to test and exmine musical phenomena do not seem to be objective in the true sense.

The perception of music as quantitative or as qualitative should be understood less as an exclusive choice than as a momentary emphasis or as a bias which is cultural. A quantitative perception is one which focusses on the intelligible phenomenon of sound and its capacity to be measured. Any approach to sound which focusses on its physical aspect shows a tendency to emphasise its fixity and this way of thinking enables one to describe sound in terms of cycles per second of frequency or durations counted by the metronome. On the other hand, the qualities of musical sound are chiefly concerned with sensual phenomena and cannot be captured in objective measurements. There is no way of labelling the sensation of musical tones as they are experienced by the performer and the listener. A quantitative focus on a melody reveals only that certain frequencies occurred for certain durations but the character and colour of the sounds can never be measured since they are the experience and feelings of the performer.

It is obvious that testing and examining of musical facts have limitations to a certain extent and can never be taken as objective. Music is neither an unarticulated aural sensation perceived all at once nor a structured skeleton built up over the time, it is both. The western methodological developments which are described as scientific methods help one to be "objective" but the results are always inter subjective in musicological research. Ethnomusicology distinguishes itself as a different discipline from Musicology mainly by its methodology which emphasises the study of Music with a "Scientific" method and socio-cultural perspectives.

CHAPTER III

Ethnomusicology and Folk Music Research

The study of Ethnomusicology began with the study of the Folk musics. Documentation is one of the main areas of study in Ethnomusicolgy as the discipline gives importance for Field work and use of the field techniques in the research methodology to study Music. "Ethnomusicology is an approach to the study of any music not only in terms of itself but also in relation to its cultural context" (Hood; 1969) This aspect of the discipline focusses more on the study of Folk Songs and Folk musical instruments.

In India, not much attention was paid to study Folk Musics of India before Independence. The first Indian scholar who took an interest in studying the Folk songs was Rabindranath Tagore. The folk songs collected by Rabindranath Tagore were published in a monthly magazine called "Sadhana" from 1899.

It is interesting to find that research in Folk Music was first undertaken by British scholars who were the employers of the British Government in India.

In 1817, charles E. Grover first published a collection of 79 songs with English transliteration and translation with the title "The Folk Songs of South India". Later James Abbot, Richard C. Temple, George Grierson, W. Crooke, R.E. Enthonem, W.C. Airoher and

Verrier Elwin published articles on the Folk musics of India in the Journal of the Royal Asiatic Society of Great Britain and Ireland and in the Royal Asiatic Society of Bengal from 1820 - 1920. Their attempts were not on a research study of Folk Music but only a compilation of the collected Folk Songs material from secondary sources, and translations of the text in English with transliteration. They resorted to Arm-chair method of Field work and the material was gathered by their Indian subordinate employees and translated by them into English. Mr. G.A. Grierson who has published an article on "Some Bihare Folk Songs" states. "The Following songs ... were collected by me when acting as a Magistrate of Patna. They were written down for me by Babu Shiv Nandan Lal Ray, Deputy Magistrate. The great preservers of these songs are all the women of all classes and it is therefore possible for a European to obtain them directly from their store keepers ... doubly indebted to Babu Shiv Nandal lal Ray, who has given me these songs ..." (p.6).

Later when Indian scholars took up research on Folk songs, they followed the methodology of the predecessors, the British scholars in compiling the collection of Folk song material and their translation. According to Indian scholars Folk songs are spontaneous outpourings of the joy and sorrow of the people and Folk Music does not have any rules in the construction of text and tune.

Mr. Sankar Sen Guptha established the Indian Folk lore society in Calcutta and Mr. K.D. Upadhyaya founded the Indian Folk Culture Research Society in Allahabad in 1960s. Mr. Sen Guptha remarks that "Indian Folklorists in most cases have deviated from just treatment of the subject ... they are lying too, much stress on the literary value of the folk song. But the thing is that its soico-historical, and psychological values merit more attention than its literary value, Little has been attempted by way of studying folk music with a musicological approach ..." (p.6-7) None of the Indian scholars who have studied Folk songs of India have said that Folk songs are not spontaneous outpourings and they have grammar or rules of their own in the text and tune, The text of the folk songs no doubt have a very clear structure as a compositional form and a clear identifiable melodic pattern. Instead of mere collection and cataloguing of folk songs, analytical study of folk songs needs to be made to find out their compositional rules in the text and melody. They are more improvised in the text part as well as in the melody part than classical music and innumerable Folk songs keep coming up everyday from the People.

Though the term "Folk" may be applied to humanity in general, it is always used to denote the illiterate people of the villages and rural areas. Their compositions and their way of performance voice and instrument - are not cultivated in the same way as done for the Art music. It may be said that Folk songs are composed at different contexts and they are perfectly suited only for those occasions for which they are composed. They are learnt orally by the performers and many times the performer is the composer of the Folk song.

Of late American Ethuomusicologists have taken up research studies on Indian Folk songs and they adopt the Ethnomusicological methodology which brings forth enormous information of the folk melodies and how culture has a direct influence upon music. The method adopted for collecting Folk songs and other materials are scientific as they use modern field techniques in their field work for Documentation. The analysis of the text and tune of the Folk melodies becomes more objective as the documentation work is done with precision.

Documentation of Folk songs and musical instruments:

The term document means any kind of recorded information which will furnish evidence. Documentation therefore ensures a recorded evidence by its writings, printing or audio-visual recordings or films. In olden days, a document was in the form of a paper written or printed but with the advancement of science and technology, audio-visual representations are considered as a more valid documents. Documentation requires a specialist, the documentalist to assemble, classify and organise the documents with a systematic approach. The Ethnomusicologist learnt to be a documentalist before he starts to do research study. Documentation which is one of the tools in the scientific methods of research is used in Ethnomusicoloy for the study of Folk and Tribal music of any culture with precision using the audio-visual aids besides using written medium. The system of documentation involves in collecting the data with relevant particulars and also in sorting and classifying these data in an organised method.

"Folk music is considered as a social phenomenon, having a certain function in human life; therefore it has to be observed and referred to in its context" (Brailoiu; 1970). Regarding music as an event occuring in various contexts, the documentation is prepared analysing the events (social/ritual) and the components of the context of the immediate situations as observed by studying

1. Participants
2. Relevant actions

3. Relevant musical instruments
4. Music in terms of melodic analysis and the analysis of song texts

Documentation is also made on the general context of culture by examining

1. Different occasions of performance and the values in terms of which they take place
2. The relationship of musical events with other respects of culture
3. Factors which affect the musical practice through acculturation

Since objectivity in collectin the data at the source is emphasized, the tool kits such as Tape recorded, Cameras, Video and Movie Cameras are used to record the events but the texts of the songs will be written on paper with translation on the spot in order to study the recorded material with accuracy. Prof. Bruno Nettl emphasised the necessity of using the mechanical devices for recording by referring to the apocryphal story of the anthropologist who learnt an Australian aboriginal song and practiced it on the long voyage back to Europe, making such changes in it (presumably unconsciously) that it was transformed into a German Folk Song. Therefore the collection of songs, instrumental music with their context needs to be made with the use of mechanical recordings, the audio-visual mediums which would provide an accurate record of the music or the melody and rhythm, intonation and ornamentation besides a reproduction of the style of the performers movements which cannot be reduced to notation.

There are two methods of Recording (1) **Actuality recording** which is the recording of the event as it actually takes place. It is a plain non-analytic record aimed at capturing the atmosphere of the occasion. It is particularly valuable as a document of music performed at social and religious rituals.

The other is **Interview recording** which is a recording made under the specific facts required by the collector to know more about certain details of an Actuality recording.

During documenting the performance, the entire song should be recorded since most singers make minor variations in the tune or melody in the different stanzas though the basic melody of the first stanza is repeated for the following stanzas. The text should be written down at the time of the recording itself as the wcrds may not be intelligible at the record when it is sung by the performer. Also it is important to get a translation of the text while in the field itself as some of the dialects can be translated accurately only by the performer. When the songs are part of a myth or story, it is better to get as much of the spoken context as possible.

In the case of instrumental music, the notes produced with the open strings of the instrument, the basic pitch of the wind instruments and in the case of drums whether they are tunable or non-tunable and their basic strokes need to be recorded separately. In recording an ensemble, making the recording with all the instruments played together and then without stopping the machine moving the microphone nearer to each performer or with string or wind or percussion groups and recording the music as it sounds give an idea of how the tone qualities of the different group of an instrumental ensemble is mixed together besides helping to transcribe the role of the particular instrument or group's melodic part.

Identification of the recording in the Field work is very important. An unidentified recore is almost of no value for any purpose. It is essential to make the identifications at the time of recording itself to ensure that there is no omission in the subsequent identification on the record. The field worker must give these identification directly through the microphone which should go along with with the recorded material.

1. Date, month, year and time of the day
2. Particulars of song and instrumental music
3. Context of the performance
4. Particulars of the performer and
5. Particulars of the instruments and instrumental playing

After the materials are gathered with proper identifications, the second part of documentation which is the most important for Archiving or Research begins. This part is worked out with a system of assembling the material and radical interpretation on the acquired material.

The first important process is the notation and transcription of the folk songs and melodies from the Folk instruments. This part is almost neglected in the documentation procedure of folk songs/musics since most of the researchers in folk music are Anthropologists and Folklorists. Ethnomusicology stresses the importance of transcription and analysis in its methodological principles. With the perspective of Ethnomusicology the age long process of documenting folk musics becomes more accurate and precise by the process of transcribing the folk melodies.

The transcription can be made aurally with the help of an ethnomusicologist and may be compared with the mechanical transcriber the Melograph. A transcription is a subjective interpretation of a sounding musical phenomenon postulated objectively by its transformation coded into a graphic form. In other words, it is a graphic statisation of a dynamic sound form with its pitch rhythm and tempo. In this sense transcription is simultaneously an analysis simplified and generalised sound manifestation. This visual form of music from the folk performers enables one to evaluate them in a satisfactory way, to catalogue them with the use of classification and comparison on their 'musicostylistic' characteristion.

With the aid of the graphic transformation of the folk melodies, classification can be made on their style and structure, and their typological and variational relationships besides interregional and interethnic variations.

In the field of style and structure of the Folk songs, three parameters are considered

1. Metro-rhythmic
2. Tonal structure
3. Syllabic variety

According to the beginning of the melodic pattern, the lexicographic identification is made.

For typological purposes, two systems of classifications are adopted. First system gives the possibility of a seven stage analysis.

1. Family
2. Number of melodic sections

3. Type of syllabic structure
4. Number of syllables
5. Type of composition of measures
6. Construction of measures in the single melodic line
7. Distribution of rhythmic values in the measures.

The other identifies five elements (variants)

1. Number of melodic sections
2. Construction of measures in the sections
3. Melodic line of the single section
4. Cadential tones/phrases
5. Melodic pattern at the beginning

Later the musics will be assembled based on their geographical region and all those which belong to the same musical genre.

Another classification on the melody will consist of a list of "registry" of melodies and will prepare a classification on how many songs with different texts are performed with the same melody and how many melodies are performed with the same text (different versions of the same song).

Regarding the musical instruments, a careful study on the shape and size of the resonators and other parts of the different instrument has to be recorded through video or filming. The techniques of playing the instruments also need to be recorded through video recording or filming. A questionnaire or an interview is made to find out the personal history of the player and his role in society. About the instrument, the facts regarding the making of the instrument as well as the status of the instrument in the society and his knowledge of playing the instrument through training or from the family tradition and the history and age of the instrument needs to be recorded through tape recorder as well as with written manuscript. The systamatisation of the documented material must be also supplemented with a catalogue of information regarding the field work and field techniques that had been employed for documenting the facts.

Factors to be documented

1. Collector's Name and Address
2. Date, Day, Month & Year of Recording
3. Place (Village, Town, State & Country)
4. Context of Recording
   a. place
   b. number and name of participants
   c. voices/instruments
5. Title of the piece
   a. original language
   b. translation
6. Beginning of the piece
   a. Text and Translation
7. Language/Dialect
8. Source and age of the composition
   Source and age of the text and melody (Anoymous, Composer, author, way of transmission according to the informant).
9. Genre

10. Function and context (in connection with custom/ ceremony social/ritual)
11. Mode-Scale/tune (Rag)
12. Rhythm pattern - Triplet, Quartet etc.
13. Performer(s) name/number/Instrument/occupation/residence/place of origin.
14. Mode of Recording - a) Tape recorder b) Video c) Film
15. Quality of recording
16. Length of recording
17. Recording techniques used

    1. Analog 2. Digital 3. Video 4. Film or Movie
    a) Mono b) Stereo c) Noise reduction

2. Particulars of performers

    a) Individual performers

        1. Name
        2. Address
        3. Nationality, race, tribe or community
        4. Place of birth
        5. Approximate age
        6. Sex
        7. Occupation
        8. Education
        9. Does performer belong to a musical society
        10. Any musical training
        11. Performer's travel outside his native place

    b) Ensemble

    Particulars of the leader and notes on the history of the ensemble

Particulars of the individual players and his training and background.

Thus in the perspective of Ethnomusicology documentation is made very systematic and well organised. It consists of all relevant information necessary regarding the collection of the material be it Folk Songs or musical instruments. Today, documentation of Folk Musics or Musical instruments can be done with visual and audio recordings besides writing down the information on the field which will be accurate for research analysis of the material. The discipline Ethnomusicology emphasises the scientific methodology of documentation in the Field using the appropriate field techniques to make the research study to be more objective in the field of Folk Music Research.

CHAPTER IV

ETHNOMUSICOLOGY IN INDIA

Ethnomusicology is cultural-musicological studies of music. The Indo-British inter-relationship paved the way for cross cultural communication through music works. The new discipline Ethnomusicology emerged in India during the British period of Indian history when the Western writers began to write on Indian Music in English language.

In the history of music, the intercultural aspects of music can be found in every style of music because of the socio-cultural changes through the rulers of the different periods in a Nation's history or through cultural communications which are made by the exchange of musicians. The influence of one style of music upon the other style is called intercultural music. It can be said that all musics in the world are intercultural. The discipline Ethnomusicology studies music in the socio-culrural perspectives to understand and analyse the particular style of music. When the socio-cultural perspectives are applied to the study of music, one finds that every style of music in the world is intercultural by one reason or other. The discipline Ethnomusicology also gives emphasis for the study of music not of their own but a different music culture which promotes the intercultural perspective of music.

With reference to Indian music, the Moghul period influenced the performing style of Indian music and the

British period in Indian history influenced both the performing as well as scholastic traditions of Indian Music.

British writers on Indian Music - Birth of Ethnomusicology in India

In the history of Indian Music literature the writings of Western authors play a significant role for the emergence of a new discipline - the intercultural Musicology, the study of Ethnomusicology in India. A valuable intercultural contact began with the writings of Sir William Jones an English High Court Judge, Calcutta and an Indologist who first wrote on Indian Music with the title "On the Musical Modes of the Hindoos" presented in 1784 which was published in the Asiatic Researches, Vol.3 in 1792.

The writings of the Western authors on Indian Music were/are meant for non-Indian and Western readers and scholars. Therefore their perspectives and approaches to Indian Music became different from the Indian Writers who wrote on Indian Music for Indian scholars. Their inter-cultural approach is continued uptodate by the American and other non-Indian Ethnomusicologist who write on Indian Music mainly for their country men.

The comparative methodology of the west was first introduced by the western writers on Indian Music. The Indian musical system was compared with the western musical system is describing the solfa syllables Sa Ri Ga Ma Pa Dha Ni as C D E F G A B in which case the Middle C of the west is not equal to the **Shadja** which is the first note of the Indian music gamut. When the letter name C was used by Western writers in the works to denote the first note **Shadja**, the western scholars who are interested in knowing about Indian Music were able to understand better than what Indian authors used to write only the Indian terminologies in their writings. For this same reasons, the Western notation was also introduced in the writings of western scholars for Indian songs. One may find this practice of writing the Indian Music compositions in Western staff notation, using key signatures to denote the notes taken by the raga in the writings of Ethnomusicologists of today.

Because of the influence of the early 19th century British writers who used western staff notation for Indian music compositions, a few Indian authors such as S.M. Tagore and A.M. Chinnaswami Mudaliar brought out the Indian compositions in western staff notation in early 19th century itself. One may find the influence of the western writers' methodology on some of the Indian writers' in their works as early as 19th century.

From 1835, English language became the official language of British India and even after independence, the bilingual language policy is followed in India. According to the American Ethnomusicologist Prof. Harold Powers, the coming of English language on Indian Music literature is a very valuable illustration of intercultural contact. The information about the performing tradition and performers are documented first in the writings of the Western authors which stand as a landmark in the history of Indian Musicological approach. The Ethnomusicological methodology, began to be introduced by the Western writers for the study of Indian Music. They provide a great amount of information about the performers and their musics of that period which are missing in the writings of Indian authors who rely only upon the scholastic tradition. The information provided on the performance practice of their period. (i.e.) late 18th century and early 19th century] reveal that the Inter-cultural aspect in the performing tradition of Indian Music was also prevalent at the period. The writings of St. Meadows Taylor give us the interesting information that a Veena player from Mysore rendered a large portion of Beethoven's sonata in A major and was applauded for his effort and playing as early as 19th century. Also we come to know from the writings of Capt. Willaird that the Hindusthani Music was performed in Western musical instruments in early 19th century. (S.M. Tagore, Hindu Music 1965).

The Indo-British cross cultural communication resulted in the intercultural musicology/Ethno-musicology not only in Indian Musicological tradition but also on the performing tradition by the adoption of western musical instruments, scale-oriented Ragas based on western scales and Indian Music compositions based on Western Musical patterns and style. Attempts were/are made to compose orchestral music with Indian Music and Musical instruments such as Violin, Clarionet, Mandolin, Saxaphone, Guitar and Viola are adopted to play South Indian classical music.

Among the Western writers, many in the early 19th century have given importance for the study of musical instruments in detail including the making of the musical instruments (Mr. Francies Fowko's "Vina or Indian Lyre). The study of organology introduced by the British writers of the late 18th century became an important aspect of study for the later Ethnomusicologists, Col. French donated a collection of Indian Musical instruments accompanied with a descriptive enlarged notes full of organological and logistic-folk details by St. Meadow Taylor to the museum of Ireland in 1743, which material stands as the foremost intercultural musicological in India. The illustrations of the musical instruments and the drawing of the performer in a playing position reveal the performance mode which is very important for organology studies of Ethnomusicologists.

The information regarding the performance practice of the music of that period and the list of renowned performers at that time and the musical Forms that were in vogue at the time are presented by British writers on Indian Music which are no doubt invaluable information. Another impartant feature one may find in the essay of Mr. Fowke "on Veena or Indian Lyre" is that the informants for him to write his essay were two musicians Jeevan Shah and Pyar Khan". In the history of Indian Musicological writings the earliest reference to that of the performers to be the informants instead of the scholastic works for sources of information is an interesting factor and here, we find the methodology of Ethnomusicology being introduced. Mr. Fowke's article is also historically important in the Indian Musicological Methodology for its objective and precise writing on Musical instruments with Socio-cultural perspectives.

In Mr. William A. Stafford's "Oriental Music, the music of Hindustan or India", the historically important reference that western Violin was in use in some parts of India as far back as the early part of 17th century (222 p) is furnished, which is another invaluable information.

The writings of Mr. J.D. Patterson's "on the grammar or Musical scales of the Hindus" (Asiatic researches, Vol.9), Mr. Francies Fowke's "The Vina or Indian Lyre" (Asiatic researches, Vol.1), Captain Williard's. "On the Music of Hindustan" (1834) in the journal of Asiatic Society, Col. James Tod's "Music", Mr. George C.M. Birdwood's "The Industrial Arts of India" (1880), and Mr. R.H.M. Bosonquest "The Hindu Division of the octave with some additions to the Theory of systems of the Higher Orders" (1877) [proceedings of the Royal Asiatic Society, London], give interesting and valuable information on Indian Musicology with an outsider's perspective meaning those who do not belong to the native Indian culture. Thus the cultural contact of the Britishers gave birth to the new discipline Ethnomusicology in India.

All the above mentioned writers have written about the music of North India or Hindusthani music and titled their works as "Music of India" or Hindusthan which is a notable factor in the history of Ethnomusicology in India. Captain C.R.Day is the only British writer who has extensively devoted his work to the Music of South India and his work is an Ethnomusicological study of South Indian Music.

The next phase in the historiography of Ethnomusicology in India is that the English writers were Indian civil service officers and not musicologists! A Music diary or a trip through India was produced by Mr. A.H. Fox Strangway. Ernest Clements brought out three works, "Introduction to the study of Indian Music (London, 1913). The Ragas of Hindustan (1918) and the Ragas of Tanjore (1920) and he made the connections between the ancient Indian Theory and modern practice which were based on the acoustical studies of the late 19th century with reference to Intonation or Srutis. It may be said that an awareness for a scientific study of musicology was introduced by them on Indian musicological writings.

When the English language began to be used for writing the Indian Musicology the problems for terminologies began to appear due to intercultural communication. For example the English term Opera is not the equivalent of Indian Sangeet Natak, the orchestra is another word which is not equivalent to

Indian Vadya Brunda, the Choir is not the right terminology for Brundagana of Indian Music and there is no parallel in western music for Raga and therefore, when the English term Mode or Scale is used to denote Raga it did not represent the Indian Raga exactly. This problem entered also in to the writings of Indian writers when the English language began to be used to write about Indian music. The western writers did not understand the Indian Musical concepts clearly and therefore they used English terms with which they were familiar and the Indian writers who began to write in English followed the European writers' terminologies as they did not know western music. The western writers introduced the Glossory section to their works as many of the Indian terminologies have to be defined in English t enable the non-Indian Western readers to grasp the meaning.

There is an inevitable time lag between the performing practice or tradition and the scholarly documentation of the musical practices at any given point of time and therefore the methodology of some of the early western writers missed the nature of the oral tradition as a source of finding the facts about Music. This has become another histriographical problem of Ethnomuscological writings of Western writers. With the entrance of English language in the writings of Indian Music there came many advantages and one among them is the Intercultural exchange in methodology which resulted from the contributions of the western Ethmusicologists and later by American Ethnomusicologists on Indian Music. New methodologies cultural and scientific evolved with intercultural scholastic tradition which led to the emergence of the new discipline ethnomusicology or Inter Cultural Musicology in India.

The historical process of inter-cultural musicology can be traced from the British writers on Indian Music from late 18th century and is being continued by many American, German and French Ethnomusicologists on Indian Music.

The intercultural contacts with western writers from late 18th cont, have brought new methodological phases such as socio-cultural perspectives, use of western staff notation for Indian Music, comparative method, study of the producer of the product and their traditional practices and the study of organology which paved the way for the emergence of new discipline Ethnomusicology, in India. The American Ethnomusicologists of the present day have made further developments in the methodology by introducing.

1. Field work (learning of the music of the performing tradition from the performer besides relying on the Musicological texts).
2. Use of Transcription and analysis instead of notation.
3. Study of the Music of the immediate past and present.
4. Use of the modern scientific gadgets like audio and video recordings for accurate documentation and
5. Use of Charts and Tables in writing to be more precise and effective.

These ethnomusicological methodologies are slowly absorbed by native musicologists to write about their own Indian Music with an Ethnomusicological perspective. Thus the history of the western writers on Indian Music brought out a remarkable change in the methodology of Indian writers in English and paved the way for the new discipline Ethnomusicology. It may be said that the 19th century western methodological developments which are known as scientific methodology with its aim to be 'objective' began to be introduced in the modern English writings of Indian Music by Indian writers. It has been realised that nowadays it is not enough if the Indian writers writes about Indian Music only for Indian people as it was in the earlier days. Indian musicological writings need to reach the global community and therefore the foreign language English needs to be adopted as a medium of communication and the Ethnomusicological methodology which is a scientific methodology needs to be used by Indian writers.

Thus in the scholastic tradition of Indian Music, the cultural contacts with English writers of the West during the British rule in India paved the way for the emergence of Intercultural musicology in India as the tenets of Ethnomusicological methodology are found in their writings on Indian Music.

CHAPTER V

Western Influence upon the Music of Japan, China, India and Indonesia

The influence of one style of music upon another style is known as intercultural Music. The concept of intercultural Music is a World Wide phenomenon. This concept can be traced back from the period when man started to establish contacts with the other people outside his native land. The interaction with peoples of different cultures resulted in bringing intercultural elements in the musics of the World. The term transculturalism was coined in 1940 by the Cuban Anthropologist Prof. Qrtiz meaning transformational process engendered by cultural contact. The musical instruments, musical concepts, styles, forms and other musical factors are adopted but moulded and synthasised as if the new concept which has emerged from cultural interaction belongs to the Native Culture. "There are various stages of interaction between any two different cultures of music. There is a beginning for experimental stage during which the elements that are combined from the different source though successively realised in a new context and accepted by the members of the society to which they are presented remain disparate and are closely recognised as coming from different source. At the advanced stage at which the elements will be fused and will become an unified idiom. The elapse of time between the beginning stage and the advanced stage amounts to a long period, the contemporary society assume that the idiom they receive from the past is something that developed entirely within their society" (Euba : 1989 : 115p).

The historian Prof. Michael Edwards in his work "East-West passage: the travel of ideas, Arts and Inventions between Asia and the Western World" has observed that in the 2,000 years of cultural contact and exchange between East and West ..." it is apparent that complete idea-systems do not travel... fragments only tend to be transmitted. He further says that things objects, techniques (and the inventions) travel easily and are absorbed into their new cultural settings" (1971 : 5p). When we look at the phenomenon of the influence of the West upon the East, we can notice many fragments that have been picked up and used. These include the musical instruments, techniques and musical concepts.

The influence of the West upon the East can be studied under two broad divisions, one the scholastic tradition and the other, the performing tradition. Throughout the East, the Institutionalised Music Education, the Notation and Transcription and English writings on the traditional music of one's Native Musical System are the three major influences of the West upon the East in the scholastic tradition of Music. The adoption of Western musical instruments, Western scales, styles, concepts such as large ensemble, introducing harmony are the factors which have influenced the traditional music of the East in their performing tradition. When the music was Institutionalised in the Eastern Countries, the Western Music was introduced in the schools in many of the countries. The Ear-rote method of learning music which is the traditional method of the East in countries like China, Japan, Indonesia and India was replaced by writing down the music and group education came up instead of individual training on music. The Notation and transcription began to be used as tools for learning. When the Western scholars began to write about Eastern Music in English, the Eastern Scholars also used the medium of English though the English language does not convey the exact meanings for the vernacular terms at times. For example in Indian music the term "Orchestra" for Vadya-brunda and "Opera" for Sangeeth Natak or Geya Natakam do not convey the Indian concept of orchestra and opera. But many works on music have been published in the Eastern countries in English which are no doubt due to the Western influence on the scholastic tradition.

The two different levels at which one culture encounters and assimilates the music of another in performing tradition are:

1. The musical instruments of one culture may spread to another (They do not necessary carry elements of musical style from one culture to another)
2. Elements of Musical concepts may spread from one culture to another.

Thus the objects and concepts of the West in the form of adopting Western Musical Instruments, Harmony, large ensemble and loud music are introduced in the East in recent times.

On the performing tradition, the Western Musical Instruments, Harmony, large ensemble and loud music are introduced in the East in recent times.

On the performing tradition, the Western Musical Instruments are adopted to play Indian Music with suitable modifications on the Western Instruments to play the traditional music of India. In China and Japan, the traditional musical instruments are modified to play westernised traditional music by using western devices and increasing the number of strings and shape of the instrument. In the East, we find in Japan and China "A New" Traditional music being born which is called Shin Hogaku in Japanese and in China, the "New" traditional music in India and "New" traditional Music has not yet developed as the Western Style of music does not synthesise successfully with the traditional classical music of India which is very rich with microtones or Shrutis and Gamakas which are oscillating ornaments (a kind of vibrato) using the subtle srutis in the melodies or Ragas.

In the East, the group singing or chorus have developed widely and the choir singing paved the way for introducing harmony to Asian melodic music to make the music colourful. The concept of orchestra in the East was different in the sense it was a small ensemble which played the melodic music without a conductor. Because of the Western influence, the concept of the orchestra has changed in Asian countries and now large ensemble with loud music with the introduction of harmony have evolved and the conductor is in charge of the large orchestra.

The Japanese music has a long history of cultural encounters and the incorporation of other musical styles into their music. It can be said that Japanese have a bi-musical culture dominated by the Western style with the establishment of Western music instruction on large scale in the public schools.

The Westernization in Japanese music culture began in 1868 under the Meiji Emperor, Western music education developed through Institutions. After having studied Western Music, many Japanese musicians tried to introduce the Western musical concepts and techniques into their traditional music. Luther Whiting

Mason and Shuji Izawa founded a Music Teacher's College and their original intention was to combine the best of East and West. Therefore they introduce courses in the Institution to teach Japanese traditional musical instruments as well as western music instruments but this system paved the way to have the strong impact of influence of the Western Music over Japanese traditional music. The schools trained Japanese School songs namely Syoko a genre established over 100 years ago in Japan. According to wayo Settyuron compromises between East and West were proposed through this genre. As represented by the encounters of Mr. Izawa and Mr. Mason, Syoko retains in every respect strong influence from Western culture in Japan. It consequently changed to become a New National style or a common style of music. It is not just the school songs but has become the beloved songs of Japanese who like to sing and hear namely as a part of popular songs. Instead of the Japanese traditional music, the new traditional music-Shin Hogaku became popular among Japanese people. The Westernised traditional music and the Western music are played in the traditional Japanese musical instruments such as Biwa and Koto and these instruments are modified to perform the present day Japanese music. It formed the basis to develop Shin-Hogaku "the new traditional music of Japan" for the children to harmonise Japanese melodies which later helped the young musicians and composers of modern times to create "A New traditional Music" known as Shin Hogaku. Thus following the visit of Mr. Mason in 1880 and the subsequent establishment of Western music instruction on a large scale in the public school, the Japanese music became highly Westernized in having Choral singing, large ensembles, loud music, fast music and thick musical texture owing to the introduction of western ornamentations on the melody. Since western music played a major and dominant role in the musical life of Japan for over a hundred years, it has become inevitable that fusions are attempted with the two systems which has resulted in a "New" traditional music of Japan. The German musicians from 1872-1945 worked to create a New Japanese music!

In the 20th century when the scientific technology and culture were introduced to China, Western music began to influence Chinese Music. During the past hundred years, unprecedentedly large scale exchange and fusion are going on between Chinese traditional music and Western music.

During the first 20 years of the 20th century, China was a close neighbour of Japan and via Japanese medium lot of Western Music such as children's songs, notation, music theory and musical instruments were introduced to China. In the second stage of 20 years, various music schools were set up in Shanghai and, Beijing where Western music theories were taught. The first music college was built in Shanghai in 1927 with an education system imitating Europe. It mainly imparted the knowledge and skills of Western music which helped the Chinese musicians to introduce the Western Style and techniques into their traditional music. In the third stage from 1949-78, the influence of Western music became more wide spread. People's republic of China was founded in 1949 which opened up the prospect of musical exchange between China and the West. At this period, more conservatories of music were opened in many places with Departments in Composition, conducting, Musicology Piano, orchestration and Vocal music, symphony orchestra and opera houses, Ballet Theater and musical publications on Western music history, theory and scores helped to accelerate the influence of Western music. The fourth stage began from

1978. Modern Western Music of the 20th century has been introduced to China and studied by many Chinese musicians. The "New" Traditional Chinese Music began to be created by Chinese Composers. The composers set the Chinese words to melodies of Western songs as the first move for "New" Chinese music, they introduced harmony in Chinese traditional songs. The famous composer Xian Xinghai made great contribution to New Chinese Music from 1940 and one of his famous composition is the "yellow river cantata" wherein he systematically applied the western musical ornaments and theories. In the 1950s, the single movement, violin concerto, and the Butterfly Love which is the another famous work belong to the New Chinese music became popular. During the 1980s with the rapid introduction of modern composing skills from the West, there arose great changes in the Chinese music in the concepts of what the Chinese musicians had previously. There appeared Dodecaphonic music, and Electronic music which are composed by Modern chinese Music Composers. The Chinese Composers believed that the Chinese traditional Music has developed quickly and greatly because of the impact of Western Music. Lin Tian Hua Composed a few Erhu and pipa pieces which are in traditional Chinese Music with the combination of Western Music. He applied also the skills specially meant for violin family such as pizzicato, Tremelo, and changing of the position of Erhu playing, expansion of the range of the traditional instruments enriching the expressive capacity. As a result Erhu, which did not appeal to refined taste in the past, is now often played on the stage for a concert and has become one of the instruments in which modern Chinese youngesters want to speacialise. Pipa which has been popular in China was reframed to meet the demand of equal

Chinese Lute Pipe

Chinese Bell

temperament. The player can now use it to perform twelve tone music (Malm : 1977).

Thus the tone quality and dynamics produced by the Pipa have been greatly enhanced due to Western influences. Zheng another ancient Chinese Musical Instrument which is supposed to be invented before 2,300 years is reformed with western influence. The number of strings is increased from 13 to 25 and an apparatus which can change the tonal height is added to the Zheng. Therefore with its wide compass and increased dynamics, Zheng is able to play the modulations effectively and its expressive capacity is enriched. The Chinese Composers have composed pieces where Chinese and Western musical instruments and played together or for the performances of Chinese musical instruments accompanied by Piano. The Pipa Concerto "Sisters on the Grassland" by Wu Zuquing and Wang Yanquiao and Erhu Concerto - "The Great Wall by Liu Wenjen are some of the examples which are considered as great achievements ley Chinese musicians and Composers resulting from making use of the Western Concerto forms. In 1980s number of young Composers using the modern Western skills created "New Chinese Art Music" Compositions Zhang Qian of Beijing remarks "Reviewing the history of introduction of Western music into China in the 20th century, the impact of Western Music upon the Chinese music stinulated and encouraged Chinese composers and musicians to reform the old traditional Chinese Music and create a new style of Chinese music" (Malm : 1977).

Though the Chinese Orchestra was in existence from very early times at rituals, ceremonies and entertainment, the modern Chinese Orchestra is highly influenced by Western concepts. The late Romantic Western concept of largeness has become the norm. The first modern Chinese Orchestra in Western Format with separate section of players with different group or classification of instruments, reading the music scores written in Western notation with notation stands before them While playing, and a conductor to conduct the orchestral performance was first introduced in 1942. The first full scale modern Chinese Orchestra of the People's republic was associated with the Radio Station. The modern Chinese Orchestra is divided into four sections based on the Western concept as Bowed Strings, Plucked strings, wind and pereussion instead of strings woodwind brass and percussion.

The influence of western music on Indian Music began from 18th century. Since the Britishers entered India through the Madras Port and established their first business and commercial contacts in South India, the music of South India absorbed more of the western musical instruments and also western musical concepts. They are synthasised in such a manner, the transculturation totally fused into the Native culture. The western musical instruments such as violin, clarinet, Harmonium, Saxaphone, Mandalin, Viola and Guitar are adopted and the Karnatic music in its prestine purity is played on these western instruments. These western instruments are modified in many cases to be suitable for playing the traditional Karnatic music. The Violin was first by Baluswami Dikshitar in 1796 and Karnatic music was played on this western instrument. Today, violin has become an indispensable accompaniment for Karnatic music concerts besides its potentiality as a solo instrument. The clarinet was first introduced in the Bharatnatyam recitals in the place of Mukhavina in the late 18th century first by Mahadeva Nattuvanar. Today, the clarinet has become a full fledged karnatic music instrument to perform solo music concerts with Tavil accompaniment. The other instruments such as viola, Saxaphone, Mandolin and Guitar have also become "Indianised" Western Musical instruments following the footsteps of Violin and Clarinet in the realm of Carnatic Music.

The emergence of brass band to play Karnatic music in the processions as well as Solo performance at open air is an interesting phenomenon from 18th century because of the British rule in India. The brass band musicians chose the suitable compositions for their instruments from the repertoire of Karnatic musical compositions. The Madras Corporation Band is a famous brass band troupe which used to play every day at the Marina Beach Madras for the entertainment of the public. They played only the compositions which belong to classical music.

The influence of the West upon South Indian music also brought forth new musical forms such as

"Nottuswara Sahithyam" which were composed by Muthuswami Dikshitar and "Note" by Muthaiah Bhagavatar. It is said that the Nottuswara Sahithyas are composed by Muthuswami Dikshitar when Mr. Brown, the then Collector of Madras requested him to compose Sanskrit Texts for Western airs. There are thirty six songs of the Nottuswara variety by Dikshitar but they did not become popular on the concert platforms. The Form "Note" does not have any Sahithya or Text but sung in Solfa Syllables and are set in the scale of Sankarabaranam with the accidentals. It does not have the sections as Pallavi, Anupallavi and charanam and sung as a continuous song but ending with the first line of the composition. A very popular "Note" composition is "English note" composed by Muthaiah Bhagavathar which is sung at the end of Carnatic Music concerts.

The Manipravala Text or the Text in two or three languages began to be used in musical compositions during 19th century. With the use of English and Telugu as Manipravala a Jawali has been composed in the early 19th century in the Raga Karaharapriya alternating the Telugu Text with English by Sivaramaiah.

Raga Karaharapriya : Tala : Adi

Pallavi

Oh my lovely Lalana Elane Pommanti

Charanam

1. Ituvanti Step Is it fit to take?
   Sit a while here, let me convince you

2. Evari Vaddanu Don't be angry
   Sivaramune Padamulu Padu

Composer : **Sivaramaiah**
19th Century

Besides these musicals forms, many scales are worked out based on the Western Scales and compositions are composed on these scales to make the scale attain the status of a Raga by many composers.

Examples

Garudadhvani

SRGMPDNS	- Ascending	Notes of Major scale
SDPGRS	- Descending	

Katanakutuhalam

SRMDNGPS	- Ascending	Notes of Major scale
SNDPMGRS	- Descending	

Mahati

SGPNS	- Ascending	Major chord with
SNPGS	- Descending	Dominant 7th

In the scholastic tradition, a few Western notation symbols were introduced by Subbarama Dikshitar in his work Sangitha Sampradaya Pradasini to write down the musical compositions in the early 20th century. The Indian Music Compositions in Western notation was also published by M.Chinnaswami Mudaliar in the late 19th century but they were not followed seriously by the later musicologists or musicians as the Western staff notation could not represent Indian music even to a fair amount. Of late, the research scholars in Indian music go for the scientific method for which transcription and analysis are used as tools for the scientific study of music to undertake stylistic analysis of composers and performers. The Western Methodological Development of the late 19th century which is known as the scientific method is adapted by Ethnomusicologists in India in their research on stylistic analysis.

In Northern India, the harmonium came to be in use with the influence of the Western accordion. The Robindra Sangeeth of Bengal can be said to have the Western influence as these compositions are composed in such a way that would give scope for harmonisation. Most of the Tagore songs are perormed with the Piano accompaniment and Arnold Bake, the Dutch Ethnomusicologist published 26 songs of Tagore in Western Notation to enable the performer of Piano to play the songs in 1935.

In Indonesia, the Western influence upon their music can be said as minimum though steadily it is increasing. They have the small ensemble and large ensemble and their "Gamelon" orchestra developed fully with more freedom for the artists and their tone colour is soft in Javanese orchestra and loud in Balinese orchestra. They have already the chorus in their musical concept. The Gamelon's polyphonic stratification did not follow the Western Harmony. It can be said that the western influence is seen in their scholastic tradition and in the time duration of their performances. The traditional gamelon used to play throughout the night for the Wayang Kulit theater for nine hours and due to Western influence gamelon orchestra play for short duration with specially composed short pieces for special occassions. The Western staff notation is used by number of Indonesian musicians instead of the traditional number notation as the Western music is taught in public school. Also Indonesian music in notation have been published in Western staff notation by the Western ethnomusicologists who studied Indonesian music at the Universities in USA, UK and Australia, Thus Western notation has become popular in Indonesia. For social functions, the gamelon plays for a duration of 30 mts. to 1 hour which may be described also as one of the Western influences. The principle of orchestration termed as polyphonic stratification supports the group improvision of about 30 instrumentalists, a male chorus of approximately 15 and three female soloists in realizing a complete musical fabric of as many as 25 distinct strata of sound features in the Indonesian Gamelon. It seems that since the concept o chorus and orchestra have developed already in a different manner from the west the Indonesian music has absorbed minimum of the western musical concepts in orchestraction. In modern times, we find the fusion of western musical instruments with the gamelon orchestra heading towards Avante - Garde Music.

Thus the concept of the interculturalism due to the influence of one culture upon another is a world-wide phenomenon. All known styles of contemporary Art Music Cultures that exist in the world is intercultural. When we look at music 'in' and 'as' culture or music as one of the behavioral patterns of human race one can understand the concept of interculturalism in music which results from interaction with people of different cultures. The influence of the west can be found throughout the East in their musics but the difference lies in the degree and level of Westernization.

CHAPTER VI

Intercultural Aspects in the Classical Musics of India

The intercultural aspect in music is a worldwide phenomenon. This concept can be traced back from the period when man started to establish contacts with the other person outside one's native land. The interaction with peoples of different cultures resulted in bringing the intercultural aspects in the musics of the world.

In the Classical Musics of India, the intercultural aspect has been fused in such a way that the other musical idioms have become unified with the native idiom. The Indian classical Music have two broad systems, the North Indian Music or the Hindusthani Music and the other, the South Indian Music or the Karnatic Music. Besides these two main systems, there is another music system known as Syfyana Kalam, the Classical Music of Kashmir.

According to early Music Historians of India, there was only one system of classical Indian Music throughout India which was called Hindu Music upto 14th century A.D. The bifurcation of Hindustani and Karnatic systems emerged after 14th century A.D. The musical influence of Persia and Arabia is found profusely in the classical music of North India or Hindusthani Music of today. The well known musical instruments such as Sarod Sitar and Tabla, the Musical forms such as Khyal, Thumri, Dadra and Tarana, the ragas such as Piloo, Yemen, Pahadi, Sindhu bhairavi, Zillaf-Kafi and many more ragas of the present day are the results of intercultural contacts of Persian and Arabian rulers in the past from 14th till 19th century A.D. When the Hindu Kingdoms in the North India were under the rule of the Moslem rulers they brought their court musicians to India from Persia and Arabia. The elements of the music of Persia and Arabia have integrated with the native music of India and have become a single unit of musical system known as Hindusthani Music. Thus the classical music of North India underwent many changes during the Mogul rule and the Islamic influence on Hindu Music can be seen in the musical Forms, Ragas & Instruments. The music of the Islamic countries such as Afghanisthan, Turkey, Iran, Iraq and Saudi Arabia sounds as Hindustani music for a lay Indian listener because of the intercultural influence in the Music of North India. Though the theoretical tradition of Hindusthani music speaks about the Raga-Ragini systems, Prabhandas and Tala system of Hindu tradition, the performing tradition of Hindusthani music is highly influenced by the musics of West Asia especially - Persia and Arabia.

The forms Khyal and Thumri which are the soul of Hindusthani Music's performing practice are the contributions of Moslem composers and Royal composers of Mogul Raj - such as Nizamudin Olia, Amir Khusru and Wajid Ali Shah. Interestingly the text of the song forms are not in Urdu and they speak about the deeds of the Hindu Gods such as Radha and Krishna or Shiva and Uma or Ram and Sita. They are either in Hindi or Braj Bhasa. The Ragas used in Khyals resemble much of the melodic patterns used in Maquams and Dastagh. Most of the male singers and instrumentalists of North

India are Moslems even today. The Sitar and Tabla, the two well-known and popular instruments of Hindusthani music have been adopted from Persian and Arabian music cultures. The Urdu gazals are performed at the end of Hindusthani Music concerts. The Gazal composers are Moslems and the text is not in praise of Hindu Gods. Mirza Galib is one of the famous composers of Gazals. These Gazals are performed by Hindu musicians and appreciated by Hindu listeners.

With reference to the three popular Hindusthani-musical instruments Tabla, Sitar and Sarod one may find a very good example of the concept of intercultural aspect in the classical music of North Indian Music, wherein the instruments have been adopted as Indian Instruments and Indian system of music is played by both Hindu & Moslem artists. The term Tabla is traceable directly to the Arabic "Tabl" a generic term meaning drum. The instrument came into the field of Hindusthani music only between 1750 and 1850 when Khyal and Tumri forms developed as Vocal music forms with the advent of Mogul rulers. The introduction of the Sitar to Indian Music is attributed to the Persian musician and poet Amir Khusru from Persia. He was an accompalished Persian Musician who came during the time of the rulers Khiljis and Tughlakhs of Delhi Sultans and introduced several Persian elements into Indian classical music and one among them is the Sitar. He introduced the Persian Setar which had three strings. In the Moghul paintings of the 16th and 17th century, the instrument setar is found. Later in the late 18th century the Indian Sitar emerged as seven stringed instrument with the fusion of Persian culture. The instrument Sarod originated from the Rebab which is an instrument from the Middle East. The Performers of North Indian classical music are mostly Moslems and some of them are the descentdents of the great musicians who were brought by Mogul Kings during 17, 18 and 19th Centuries. One of them is the famous, Sarod player of today Ustad Amjad Ali Khan.

Sufyana Kalam the Classical Music of Kashmir

Kashmir is located in the Western Himalayas and was under the influence of many cultures mainly those of India, the Near East Central Asia and the West. Kashmir was an active centre for Sanskrit Studies and produced a large number of great sanskrit scholars including Bharata Muni, the author of Natyasasthra, the first work on Indian dramaturgy and Music.

The Islamization was accomplished gradually through the Moslem Missionaries and Sufis who migrated from persia and Turkey. Kashmir stands as an example for Intercultural synthesis of Hindu and Islamic cultures which resulted in the intercultural Music par excellence. The period 1420-1470 which was under the rule of Sultan Zainul Abidin is considered as the Golden age as the Arts, Music, Dance and Paintings flourished under his patronage.

Sufyana Kalam or Sufyana Musiqui is the Kashmiri musical which genre belongs to classical type of music. The Sufyana Kalam has deep roots in the North Indian classical (Hindusthani Music) tradition but influenced by Central Asian Musics, Instead of Rag, the Persian Maqams are used. The principal scale of Sufyana is the Diatonic Major (Bilaval That of Hindustani Music) The entire modal system is organized in six Ahangs or families. The theory of Maquam follow the persian music theory but the performers identify the name of the Maquam with the name of the Hindusthani Rag. For example Uchuk Maquam as Rag Kalyan. The Hindusthani Time theory of Rags are followed for the Persian maquams in the Sufyana music.

Sufyana Kalam is Vocal music sung in Chorus with four to seven musicians and all sing in unison. The poetry associated with Sufyana is in Persian and Kashmiri, Urdu, Hindu and Panjabi languages. The Sufyana music is composed and the particular poem is performed in different Maquam and different Tal. they have two sections in the form as one finds in the Khyal of Hindusthani music but with on instrumental part Waqf which one finds in the near Eastern style.

There are four instruments associated with the Sufyana and among these three of them are Near Eastern origin-santur, Setar (not Sitar) and Saz-a-Kashmivi (a spiked-bowed lute and a Hindusthani traditional instrument the Dokra, a set of Tabla.

Thus Sufyana Kalam is an interesting synthesis of various styles of classical music and stands as a good example of intercultural music of India. Sufyana Kalam has an unique rhythm pattern where the names of the Talas are from Hindusthani Music (North Indian Classical) and Persian Music.

The Folk Music of Kashmir also has the influence of Afghanisthan and Persia besides the Hindu musical traits. Kashmir music in India has a great tradition of intercultural music in India due to the Hindu Moslem Cultural Synthesis.

With reference to the classical music of South India or Karnatic music, the impact of Western music is found from 18th Century onwards. It does not have any Mogul influence. The Britishers entered India through the Madras Port and started their business and commercial contacts first in South India. No doubt, the English language as well as the Western culture and music western were adopted more by the south Indians than by North Indians. The Western influence on the South

Indian music can be found in the adoption of the Western musical instruments such as Violin, Viola, Clarionet, Saxaphone, Mandolin, Guitar and also the Western Brass Band to perform Karnatic music. The song forms such as "Nottuswara Sahithyam" and "English Note" reveal the impact of westernization on Karnatic music.

The violin was introduced under the name of Fiddle in South India as many Irish Fiddlers were in Madras. Baluswami Dikshitar who was the brother of Muthuswami Dikshitar studied violin from an English Band Master at Fort St. George at Madras and adopted the instrument to play Karnatic music.

When the South Indian music composer Muthuswami Dikshitar came to Madras from Tiruvarur an interior town in South India, he listened to the Western Brass Band and got inspired by the western melodies. Mr. Brown, who was the then Collector of Madras requested this composer to contribute sanskrit text to the Western Airs such as "God save the King". The composer readily accepted and wrote sanskrit texts for western tunes and named them as "Nottuswara Sahithyae". Note is the English word which is used as a sanskritised word with Swara in the word Nottuswaram. The text "God save the king" was replaced by sanskrit text meaning let the Goddess of music save me as "Santatam Pahimam Sangeeta Syamale".

The "Nottuswara Sahithyas" are intercultural musical compositions by Muthuswami Dikshitar who is one of the greatest composers of South India Classical Music. He lived in late 18th and 19th Centuries. In these compositions, the melodies are from the Western music compositions. The title of the European song is mentioned to identify the melody and they are composed with Sanskrit Text.

A few examples are the following:

1.	Jagadeesa Guruguha	- Lord Macdonald's Reel
2.	Kancheesam Ekambaram	- Country Dance
3.	Peetavarnam Bhaje - Taza	- Ba - Taza
4.	Raja Sri Venkataraya	- March
5.	Ramachandram	- "Let us lead a life of Pleasure."
6.	Sakalasuravinuta	- Quick March
7.	Sakthi Sahita Ganapathim	- Voluez Vous - Dancer?
8.	Santatam Pahimam	- God save the King/ Queen
9.	Souri Vidhinute	- "Oh Wistle and I will come to you, my lad".
10.	Sriranga Harikripa	- Moll Rowe (Moore)
11.	Vande Minakshi	- Lime rick
12.	Varalila Gana	- Marl broock.
13.	Varamangal	- Marl broock.
14.	Varasiva Balam	- Castilian Maid (Moore)

(Introduction by John Marr (U.K.) for the book "The European Airs of Muthuswami Dikshitar" Ed. by Mr. R. Sankaramoorthy, p.XI - XII)

Today, one finds that violin is an indispensable accompanying instrument of Karnatic Music besides its potentiality as a Solo instrument to play Karnatic music. The clarinet was also introduced to Karnatic music during 18th Century as an accompaniment to Bharatanatyam (classical dance of South India) concerts. The clarinet is now used also as a solo instrument to give Karnatic music recitals. The clarinet is accompanied by the ancient drum Tavil which is the accompanying instrument for Nagaswaram, an ancient oboe type instrument of South India. The musical sound of clarinet is made to resemble the Nagaswaram the Indian oboe, by introducing certain changes on the keys.

From 18th Century onwards the Western Brass Band is used to play Karnatic music during wedding procession along with the traditional Nagaswaram band which emphasises the concept of intercultural aspect in the music of South India. The brass band players play the compositions in the ragas of Karnatic music.. The other western instruments such as Viola, Saxaphone, Mandolin and Guitar are adapted to perform Karnatic music and they have become very popular. The players on these instruments are respected equally with the performers who play the traditional South Indian instruments such as Vina, Mrudangam and Flute.

The impact of Western Music upon South Indian Music began from 1798 during the rule of King Sarafojee. The King had organised the Tanjore brass band for the first time and also collected western musical instruments like Violin, Clarinet, Dulcimer, Piano German flute, Tambourine and harpsichord to play the western tunes on them in a group as an orchestra, (Lord Valenia's Travels, p.360). The king himself learnt western music, copies of note books containing songs in western staff notation and the theory explained in a lucid manner by Thomas Chapman and copied by W. Holdworth "for His majesty the Raja of Tanjore" with the date 1.3.1775 are available in the Tanjore library archives. There are other note books in which the staff notation has been explained, with Devangari letters for representing Solfa names. [Guide to the records of Tanjore, Vol.V].

In the classical music of South India, the Hindusthani ragas such as Hindusthani Behag, Hindusthani Kafi, Sindhubhairavi, Jonpuri, Bageshri, Desh, Kalavathi, Tilang are adopted in the musical compositions, as well as in the improvisatory parts of Ragas and Swara improvisation from 18th Century onwards. The Bhajans which are composed in the language of North India known as Braj Basha and which are in Hindusthani ragas are invariably performed at the end of a classical music concert of South India, today.

Thus one may find the intercultural aspects profusely in the classical musics of india resulting from cultural interaction.

The interculturalism in the North Indian classical music or Hindusthani music occurred with the result of invasions. The cultural interaction was brought by the kings and their retinue of court musicians and intercultural aspect in South Indian Music was brought by British Rulers who came with the intention of doing business in India and later became the rulers. They also brought with them Western musicians from their country who influenced native musicians to learn Western music and western musical instruments.

The intercultural aspect in Music springs forth from cultural interaction. The musical instruments, the musical, concepts the musical forms, rhythm and other musical factors are adopted but moulded and synthasised as if the new concepts which have emerged from cultural interaction belong to the native culture. Interculturalism is synthesis of the musical cultures which results in transculturalism. The term transculturation was coined by a Cuban Anthropologist Prof. Qrtiz in 1940 to mean that the transformational process engendered by cultural contact. American Ethnomusicologist Alan Merrian's concept of looking at the Music "in" and "as" culture helps one to understand the concept of intercultural aspect in Musics is the fundamental concept for the present day Avant-garde music.

It may be said that the modern trends in intercultural aspects in the Classical Musics of India are

1. An increased number of non-Indians' interest in learning Indian Classical Music in India and Overseas.

2. Performance of Indian Music by non-Indians with mastery in overseas and teaching of Indian Music in the Universities by non-Indian Scholars at overseas.

3. Increase in the number and output of western composers in using Indian melodies and musical instruments in their new creation of Avant-grade music presentations and

4. Increase in the number of adapting western musical instruments to perform classical music of India such as Saxaphone, Mandolin, Guitar and Viola in 20th Century.

Intercultural aspects in the Education of Indian Classical Music

The present era is an important turning period in the world music education with the rapid intercultural exchange of techniques and concepts. The music educators are challenged in transmitting the music culture to the students in the Institutions as well as those students who take up private study and who are foreign to the music culture which they are going to study. The rapid expansion of scientific technology after the World War II made the music travel from Continent to Continent via Recordings, Films, Radio and Television which created interest in many to learn other styles of music. In this setting, one of the advantages of interculturalism in music education is the emergence of new concepts in Music education evolved by the teachers with their practical experiences.

New concepts have emerged in teaching Indian Classical Music to teach non-Indian students who are not exposed to Indian culture.

Transmission of Music culture refers to

> "the means whereby the knowledge, traditions, ideas and cumulative musical creations of a society are passed on from generation to generation (including) those 'idioms' of musical culture which are not self propagating but demanding conscious learning of a wide range of materials and skills which cannot be acquired by the individual in the normal process of enculturation."

(Nketia J.H. Kwabena; "Music education in Africa and the West" in Education and Research in African Music, Lasaka, 1975, 8 p).

With reference to the teaching of Indian music two types of situations are present with the advent of interculturalism.

1. Indian Music teacher with his/her non-Indian students outside India.
2. Indian Music teacher with his/her non-Indian students in India.

The non-Indian students take up their music education.

1. At the Institutions in India and Overseas.

2. Private study with the Indian teachers in India and Overseas. The goals or aims of the non-Indian students to study Indian Music are different from Indian students in most cases. According to the purpose of their study, the syllabus for teaching are prepared. The aims of the non-Indian students to learn Indian Music are mainly.

1. To undertake research on the music culture and bring out a publication to enable his/her countrymen to get to know about the concepts of performances and theory of Indian Music.

2. To teach Indian Music in the conservatories in their Country, where there are Ethnomusicology of World Music programs at the University level.

3. Composers who wish to write compositions on the concept of interculturalism.

4. Very few like to become performers of Indian music but upto date none of the non-Indian students have settled in India to take up Music performance as their career.

The years of study by non-Indian students to become proficient in Indian Music are also very limited. The researchers who come to India to write about Indian Music for their doctoral or post-doctoral work undergo private study with Indian music teachers and spend minimum six months and maximum three or four years. The non-Indian students who are already Music educators in conservatories and who are asked to equip themselves to teach Indian music in their Ethnomusicology program, study Indian Music in Music

Institutions and sometimes with private teachers. They come under study grants but it is limited for a short period such as six months upto one year. The composers of new intercultural music also spend only a short period of time to learn Indian music to understand the concepts of Indian music.

The other class of non-Indian students are those who takeup Indian music in their core curriculum in the Universities or College in overseas and study from the rudiments of Indian Music upto the singing of the compositions. Since their repertoire of compositions is very limited during their course of study for four to six semesters. They are not able to do full justice in performance. They are unable to master the creative part of the performer's aspect in Indian Classical Music.

Although the tradition of Indian Music is historically unique, the problems with the advent of interculturalism are universal. The music educator has a challenge to device new methods of teaching Indian Music efficiently within a short time and for the students of different aims and who are also do not belong to Indian culture to understand the philosophic and socio-cultural norms of Indian Music.

The new devices which are the outcome of interculturalism in Indian Music education are the following:

1. Notation - Staff notation along with Indian Sargam notation.
2. Transcription of the ornaments used on the notes with the use of microtones.
3. English terminologies for the technical words of Indian Music.

4. Audio - Visual equipments to record the classrooms lessons.

5. Listening Sessions - to listen the music of the great masters for many hours to prepare the student to reproduce the musical style more effectively and also to train their ears to appreciate Indian Music.

6. Visual sessions with videos to understand the cultural and social background of the performance of Indian Music.

7. Using the comparative method of teaching to make the student understand the concepts of Indian Music in a better way.

8. Teaching the pronounciation of the text which are in Indian languages for the vocal students.

9. Translation for the text to understand the meaning of the compositions to perform with feeling.

In the traditional methods of teaching, the concepts and methods were different. The fundamental Indian philosophical concept was followed in the ancient Guru-Sishya or Gurukula Education. Music Education was valued as religious or spiritual instruction as the practice of Indian music was considered as a means for salvation Moksha.

The ideal attitude for the musician was of complete dedication with the goal being self-liberation through total identification with the Music as Yoga. It required enormous amount of time with the teacher's personal attention.

Modern social and economic conditions made it unwise for the student of music to commit so many years of his young years without any basic education with the gurukula system of learning when he cannot be certain of success in the field of music profession. Girls and women also want to learn Music. They cannot afford to stay all time in their teachers home for many years. In these circumstances the Indian music was introduced in the conservatories at private level and in public schools, colleges and universities. In the Indian Institutions, the teaching methods are structured for Indian students based heavily on the old traditional system of Gurukula system.

Uptodate the methods at the Music Institutions in India for Indian students are the following:

1. The songs are taught only with Swara Notation and many times the songs are **taught orally**.
2. The music teachers **never use transcription** to teach the ornaments that have micotonal variations. Instead of transcription, the only method adopted is **imitation**. The student is asked to **imitiate** the teacher.
3. There will not be any recording at the class room teaching session and no kind of listening or viewing sessions are included since Indian students have plenty of opportunities to listen and view the live performances.
4. The **technical words** of Indian music **are** taught is **Indian languages** and never with Western terms.

The students who wish to become techers study in the conservatories whereas the students who want to become a performer take up the study of music with great masters privately besides their study of music at the Institutions.

Since these teaching methods of transmitting music of Indian students in India fail in many aspects in teaching a non-Indian student in overseas or in India, the music education of Indian music is challenged to devise the new concepts to 'cope up' with the inter-culturalism in Music education.

The swara notation is substituted with staff notation and transcription, audio-visualaids are largely provided to understand the music effectively within a short span of time. Terminologies have been translated into English to be intelligible to the overseas students and the pronounciation of the Indian languages are taught for vocal students besides a translation of the text is provided to perform with feeling.

Music is taught with interdisciplinary approaches with the use of cognative psychology and socio-cultural perspectives.

The squating posture to perform Indian Music requires practive for the non-Indian students before they learn Indian Music. The student becomes part of the Indian culture when he learns to sit like an Indian. The interrelation between the music and cognative psychology reveals "that it seems unlikely that music could have penetrated to the core of so many different cultures unless there were some fundamental human attraction to the organised sound which transcended cultural boundaries somehow the human mind endows these sounds with significance (and) they become symbols for other than pure sound ...." No doubt most of our responses to music are learned." A person may understand the music heard without being moved by it but if moved "must have passed through the cognitive stage which involves forming an abstract or symbolic internal representation of the music. The nature of this internal representation and the things it allows a person to do with music is the central subject matter of the cognitive psychology of music". (Sloboda : 3p) This concept of the cognative psychology plays a vital role in teaching non-Indian students. The developments in the cognative psychology is used in the music education owing to the pan human aspects of enjoying music.

Thus with the advent of interculturalism in Music Education, the new methods of teaching Indian Classical Music have emerged based on cognative psychology and socio-cultural perspectives besides the traditional musical approach.

CHAPTER VII

INTERCULTURAL ASPECTS IN THE MUSICS AND THEATRES OF SOUTH EAST ASIA

The Tonal systems and the musical instruments of South East Asia reveal a high influence of Indian cultural behaviour in their music. In a broad sense, it can be said that the main tonal systems of South East Asian music is Pentatnic. But diatonic system is also used. The music is melodic which is an Asian trait and the use of the tonal systems as a mode, resembles that of Hindu and Moslem systems. The Raga and Maquam patterns are widespread in the melodies of South East Asian Music. In their Theatrical forms, they use the stories from the two great epics of India, Ramayana and Mahabharatha. The presentation methods of their theatres except phillippines, reveal the impact of Indian cultural behavioural pattern in their characters, costume, music and mimic expressions. The vocal style is influenced by Hindu and Moslem styles. In India, both the moslem and Hindu cultural traits and styles are found in North Indian music or Hindusthani music and in south Indian Music or Karnatik music respectively. Thc instruments gongs and their varieties, Rebab, Lutes and Zithers, the drums, the different variety of flutes, jew's harp and serunai are found in almost all the South East Asian countries and melodic orchestral music seems to be characteristic of south East Asian Musical culture. Many of these instruments seem to be an off shoot o the ancient Indian instruments, is held by adherents of the theory of diffusion which claims that every basic instrument type was invented only once and then spread about the world in variant forms. An opposing theory of polygenesis holds that each instrument was invented in several different places at different times, the variants of such separate inventions may or may not have overlapped as each form spread about. (Malm: 80p) So far, neither theory seems to offer the exclusive answer to the questions of relationships between musical instruments around the world and one can find examples that seem to support each argument.

Malaysia

Indigeneous Malay music are many and varied and reflect the character of the various regions of the Malay Peninsula from which they come. They have a rich musical, dance and theatrical traditions especially the northern states Kelantan, Kedah and Trengganu. The Southern States particularly those on the west coast of peninsular Malaysia show a strong bias to Western European cultures in all their performing arts. Most of the Malaysian traditional music is associated with drama and dance or with ceremonial and ritual acts involving muslim, Hindu and animistic beliefs.

In India no doubt the traditional music is associated with drama and dance as we find the evidence from natyasastra and Silappadikaram. natyasastra is a treatise in dramaturgy writen by Bharata in Sanskrit (2nd Cent. A.D.) Silappadikaram is a Tamil Epic which deals with dance, drama and music written by Ilango (2nd Cent. A.D.) Indian music is also associated with ceremonial and rituals involving Hindu, Buddha and Jains religions.

A popular drum of Malaysia is Gendang. It is a double headed barrel drum which resembles the South Indian Drum Mrdangam. They are tuned by rattan bracing. The Mridangam of South India has leather braces and the pitch varies with the tension of the braces. The player of Gendang sits with the drum resting on his left thigh or on a wooden stand and beats it with his hands. This style of sitting posture and the playing mode reminds us of South Indian drummers. Some times this drum is played with curved sticks and here the malaysian indigenous behavioural pattern in revealed.

Among the wind instruments, the Malaysian Serunai is played more or less like the nagaswaram of South India. The instrument is particularly characterised by the construction of the reed. Two double layers of dried palm leaf are attached, which is similar to the panai Olai Narukku known as seevali used in the Nagaswaram. There are usually seven finger holes and one thumb hole, in the instrument.

Among the idiophones the kesi is a pair of small cymbals with a central boss and flat rim which looks like the Jalra of South India and manjira of North India.

The royal courst of Kedh, perak, selangor and Trengganu have their own noubat band - a mark of the king's Sovereignity and part of Royal regalia. In North India the Noubat or nakkara Khana did play the same role in the Royal Moslem court. The Kedah Noubat or Nakkra Khana of Malaya consist of six instruments, a Negaa or nenssara - Kettle drum, two gendang - two headed laced barrel drum, one Nafiri - a long silver trumpet one Serunai and one suspended gong.

A clear Islamic influence is found in these Noubat ensemble connected to the courts of regional sultans.

As we find in Indian culture, the dance and theatrical arts as part of people's life - style, are very popular among Malaysian people. There are ritualistic dances and court-dances of solo and group varieties.

Ma yong is the theatre genre which includes stylized dances, solo and group singing with dramatic representation. This is akin to the dance - drama tradition of India such as Kudiyattam and Rasalila. It is more of a ritualistic performance. As in India, the dance - dramas are performed during rituals. By the middle of the 20th cent, a revival was made and ritualistic dance and drama were performed in public but with many changes in theatrical presentation. In this theatre, the entrance of the actors will be made with a musical accompaniment and a song is sung which is similar to the patra Pravesa Daru or the entrance songs in Indian Musical Theatres.

The Malaysians have thirty popular tunes which are similar to Indian folk tunes. There are specific tunes for each activity such as lullaby, or conveying message for lamenting among the poor. They also have a specific time unit which is constantly repeated resembling the Indian Tala Pattern. They sing with a highly ornamented mellismatic style in theatre where we find a similarity in Indian drama songs which are highly ornamented than concert songs, and the style is called Natya Sangeet.

Another noteworthy feature is the use of heterophonic chorus and heterophony accompanists in Malaysian music culture. This is very much like the trait of Indian musical culture whiere Indian people are used to appreciate the heterophonic character in music. A good example for heterophony is the violin accompaniment in a vocal concert in Indian classical Music.

The Martial dance, silat medon a stylized imitation of fighting and bergayang ata-ata, a dance involving self-defence, reflect the Indian cultural influences especially of Kerala and Tamil Nadu Martial dance culture.

The leather puppet theatre and the shadow puppet theatre which resemble Tolu Bommalattu of Andhra Pradesh and Nizhalattam of Tamil Nadu and Kerala and Chayanatak of Orissa are popular in the Northern States of Malaysia. Wayang Kulit in Malaysia is found in three different forms and their stories are based on the two great epics of India, Ramayana and Mahabharata which are in their local dialect. In India also most of the traditional provincial theatres use Ramayana and Mahabharata for their story which are written in their provincial dialects. A very close cultural link between India and Malaysia is seen in the theatrical forms. The dalang or the Puppetteer plays the role of sutradhara of the Indian Traditional Theatre. Similar to Indian theatre, music and dance play a vital role in Malaysian theatre.

Another interesting cultural similarity which comes out of moslem influences, is the Ghazal entertainment, which is very popular in North India. In Malasia also, the Ghazal form of singing is a favourite entertainment. The difference in Ghazal which is performed in Malaysia is with or without a singer and only by instrumentalists playing the gumbos and maruas (Xylophones and Jewsharp) and such instruments as gendang, moracas, guitars, harmonium and Tabela as accompaniments whereas in India Ghazal is performed only with singers with instrumental accompaniments Harmonium, Sitar, Sarangi, and Tabala. The form zikir of Malaysia resemble the Quawali singing of North Indian Music which has been absorbed from the Islamic culture.

Philippines

Phillippines are the islands at the Northern apex of the triangle formed by the South East Asian archipelago. In Phillippines, Islam was the only great Asian Tradition that has a significant impression in their culture. Indigenous and Islamic influenced traditions are the oldest layers in the musical culture of the philippines. The largest regional division in the philippines stylistically is that between the Northern and Southern islands. Within the Southers islands, there are additional cultural differences between Muslim influenced groups and those which have retained their indigenous religions.

The most important instruments for rituals and festivals are gongs, those of the North are flat while those of the South are bossed.

Vocal music in the North is of two types, one used in festivals and ceremonies and the other used in secular events. In rituals, the leader of the chorus will sing the song and the group will repeat the chorus part. Solo song are characterised by slides, trills and speech like techniques. In the South, vocal Music divides along cultural lines between moslem and non-moslem groups. Moslems have songs in the Near Eastern Style for their services and ceremonies. Certain aspects of this style, for instance melismatic, long phrases, smooth singing high pitch and tremelo are found. Non-Moslems use vocal music in thanks giving and during ceremonies communicating with spirits. In Mindanao there are syllabic psalm - like songs with narrow melodic ranges as well as a type of singing which has instrumental accompaniment or uses vocal techniques to imitate the drone and rhythm of the plucked strings.

The Islamic music tradition in the South is based on the indigenous vocal and instrumental tradition, musical customs, social contexts and aesthetics of non-moslems in Mindanas. A newer Islamic style superimposed on this tradition, has a specially distinct vocal style with a high tessitura a strained voice with various timbres and nasal enunciation. Islamic instrumental groups play a small gong ensemble. Gong music is performed for honouring people of their community and for proiding the proper ambience for ritual proceedings. Gongs are made out of bronze or brass having a diameter of approximately 30 cm. They produce diffused sounds without a focussed pitch. Gong ensemble in the North is sometimes combined with drums. The Topayya ensemble consists of 6 flat gongs played with palms of both hands.

Instruments found only among Islamic groups are principally

Kulintang	-	Gong-Chime
Gabbang	-	Xylaphone
Saunaj	-	Single reed aerophone
Biola	-	Violin and
Gandang	-	Two headed drum

The suspended bossed gong with wide rim which is called agung is found among both moslems and non-moslems. Kudyapi is a two stringed lute which is claimed by many to be of Indian origin. The Indian instrument was called Kachachapi Veena.

Most instruments in the South are made of bamboo either of blown, plucked or struck. The transverse flute verymuch resembles Indian Bansuri. The jew's harp kuling is yet another popular instrument of Southern Philippines. Though the technique of playing is the same as the Jew's harp of India and Indonesia, the Instrument is made out of bamboo. Its bamboo filament is vibrated by plucking in contrast to the Indian type which uses the attached string. The Indian Jew's harp known as Morsing or Mor-chang is made out of metal.

The common instruments in both North and South are transverse flutes, trumpet, bamboo zither with several strings, zither with parallel strings, bamboo mouth organ, and the cylindrical drum. Common vocal forms are responsorial singing, solo songs and epics. A study in the distribution of these South East Asian singing styles and instruments would show how they are related to each other to the other South East Asian traditions and possibly to the different periods of time. Both the Northern and Southern traditions use instruments made of Bamboo, shell, wood, skin and other materials found in the tropics. The closeness with nature is also evident in music performed in the open air. These features are seen in India and in other south East Asian musical cultures. Ostinatos are played with melodies in many instrumental ensembles and in performing musical forms which is a feature found also in Indian music performances. The flute is associated with men and zither with women. It is interesting to find that in North India there is no Bansuri artist of the female sex and the Indian women mostly prefer to play stringed instruments.

Thailand

During the past Six hundred years, Thai music has absorbed instruments and musical ideas from neighbouring cultures into its indigenous musical culture. The influences of Indian culture are also seen in Thai traditional musical instruments.

Three main Thai ensembles are

1. The pi-phat consisting of xylophones, metallophones sets of gong-kettles, hand cymbals, gong drum and the pi, a double read wind instrument.

Bunmese Harp - Soung
Pan-Asian Instrument

2. Khruang Sai - composed of various stringed instruments, the rhythmic percussion and a bamboo flute.

3. Mahori consisting of a melodic and rhythmic percussion, stringed instruments and the flute.

Of the seven available pitches, five are used at any one time to form the principal scale. Therefore Thai style of music is basically pentatonic, In another style called Mon (Mown) the other two pitches are used more freely as passing tones.

Thailand was formerly known as Siam and its music system is related to India and other South East Asian and East Asian Countries. The traditional music was always under the patronage of the royal courts. Music-has always been held in high regard and good musicians have always been respected and given titles by the King. This custom of honouring musicians with titles very much resemble the Indian culture. Music is used largely for theatre and dance in Thailand.

Among the percussion group, there are melodic percussion types like xylophones (nandi) and gong-chimes (gong circles and kettle gongs) and rhythmic percussion which are ching-small hand cymbals Taphon-barrel shaped drum, long cylindrical drum and vase shaped single handed drum.

Among the wind instruments, the bamboo flute is an important instrument. Among the stringed instruments Jakhe and the Krajappi are indigenous Thai instruments. The former is a zither with three strings plucked with ivory plectrum. Krajappi is a plucked lute with a resonating box shaped somewhat like a tortoise shell (from which the instrument gets its name) with a long narrow neck and its four strings are played with a plectrum. This Krajappi is also claimed to have its ancestor in an instrument of Indian origin known as Kachchapi vina.

Like the other Asian systems of Music, Thai system is non-harmonic. The music also has no notation system. The octave is divided with equidistant intervals and not tones and semitones. Thai music sounds to a person who is not familiar to Thai music as one long unbroken music without any sections. The instruments of fixed pitch are tuned to seven equi-distant pitches in an octave.

The main melodies of traditional compositions are of two types. Those of older compositions are simpler and based on motif. The new ones are more lyrical. The melodies are generally diatonic within the basically pentatonic framework. Thai style which is related to Indian raga from is basically modal. The other style is referred as mown style which although generally confined to five pitches of the pentatonic scale at basic structural points, uses the other two available pitches of the octave to a much greater extent in the melody. Shifting of the tonic is more freqment in Thai Style. In comparison with the music of India, the pentatonic and diatonic scales that are found in other Asian countries come within the large frame of Ragas of India. Modal shift of tonic was known to Indian. Musicologists from 2nd century A.D. as one finds in the Indian Musical tretises which were written in 2nd Cent A.D. (Silappadikaram, and Natyasasthra).

The music has great variety and often more than one mode occurs in one composition. Sometimes the mode is transferred to another pitch level and performed. This is done in South Indian music when singing in Madhyama sruthi by shifting the pitch sa to ma (C to E). Use of more than one mode in a composition is called Ragamalika in South Indian music and the Mishra ragas of North India take the shade of more than one raga.

Thai compositions which are called Ryang have motivic main melodies generally through composed music and such section is usually repeated. Some Ryang compositions are short which will take upto 10 minutes. These compositions are instrumental compositions.

The vocal compositions are Thao compositions wherein the vocal sections alternate with instrumental sections. There are hundreds of thao compositions in the Thai repertory. Vocal music uses a voice quality rich in partials with much ornamentation.

In most style the vocal lines adheres to the pitches of the fixed pitch system at structural points. Intricate ornaments are often used which involve pitches and inflections not found in the fixed pitch system. The vocal quality of singers is fairly complex, acoustically, and the tone is steady and straight like the tone produced in Indian music without any vibrato. Characteristic of Thai vocal style is the increase in the volume of Sound towards the end of the held pitch and the use of the glottal sound particularly a kind of glottal falsetto ornament at the end of the held pitch often a forth higher than the principal pitch. Thai traditional music stands as one of the high musical cultures of Asia.

Indonesia

Of all the highly diversified people that inhabit more than 3,000 islands in the republic of Indonesia, the peoples of Java and Bali have attained the richest cultural development.

The generic term gamelon includes a great variety of ensembles differing in size, function and musical

style. There are two styles of playing. One of soft style, a subtle, mystical and seemingly timeless flow of sound associated with singing and the other strong style a virile and powerfully resonant battery of sound.

The players are seated cross legged on mats which resembles the seating mode of Indian musicians. Indian influence and Brahmanical Hinduism entered Java in the first and second centuries A.D. Islam was present in Indonesia by atleast the 13th cent and was quite prevalent by the 15th cent.

In Indonesia the gamelon is a generic term for musical ensembles and the size of the gamelon may be either small or as big as having 75 players. Though gamelon is an instrumental ensemble, singing is included recently as an important part of central Java gamelon compositions. A female soloist (Pesinten) a male unison chorus (gerong) or a mixed chorus (gerong bedayan) are used and subtle handclap beats are heard in sections in some of the performances.

The most obvious instruments of a gamelon are its bronze metallophones. They fall into two basic types, those with slabs or keys and those with knobbed gongs. The saron has keys set over a box resonator. The other famous instruments are gender, gambang Kayu (xylaphone) and bonang. This belonged to knobbed gong family. Its bronze knobbed gongs are placed on ropes laced in wodden frame and are played with two padded sticks. Its fundamental function is to mark the time. The bonang holds a vital position in the joining of the music of many layers of sound into one coherent musical event. Kethuk, Kenong, Kempul and gong are the other time keeping instruments. In Java. There are two basic kinds o gamelon playing - the loud style, with an emphasis on the bronze instruments and the soft style in which the flute and the rebab take the main role. The rebab player is the leader. The kachchapi Zither is used in Java which is claimed as an off shoot of kachchapi vina of India. There are several different Kinds of javanese Zithers called Kachchapi.

Throughout Indonesia there is an endless variety of gamelon. In addition to many different kinds of ensembles there are a variety of musical forms. Most of the forms in Indonesian Music however are the tales of the hero panji and the local versions of the Hindu Ramayana and Mahabharata. These stories have been preserved primarily through the oral traditions of the theatre and solo songs as well as in Orchestral and dance pieces. The wayang kulit, or the shadow puppet theatre is a popular form of theatre. The puppetteer or dalang recites entire dialogues to the accompaniment of an instrumental ensemble.

The most general Javanese term for composition is Gendhing (gending). There are two basic scales in Java, the five tone slendero and the seven tone pelog. Both slendero and pelog are composed of nonequidistant invervals. The slendero scale has three modes called patet Nem, patet Sanga and patet manjira while pelog has four modes patet lima, patet nem, patet barang and patet manjira. Each patet, like ragas of Indian music is fixed to be best suited to the given mood, function, and time of the day. Attempts have been made to link south East Asian tonal systems with those of India by comparing Indian ragas with specific South East Asian scales, particularly those used in Hindu oriented theatrical religious pieces. The existence of certain beliefs concerning the mood of each scale also implies such a relation. In addition, some South East Asian musics use special ornaments on specific notes in each scale much like those of India - (William Malm; music cultures of the pacific the Near East and Asia).

ın Bali, a number of musical instruments depicted in the bas-reliefs of early Hindu - Javanese monuments have survived. Today Balinese Hinduism is practived as a way of life by a communal society in which the former royal patronage of the arts has been largely replaced by that of the village community. Temple festivals and rites of passage demand the fullest participation by musician and dancers. In the context of religious worship, the music, dance and theatre flourish, which is similar to Hindu concept,

The time theory of the nodes are strictly followed at certain times of the day or night and specific time periods especially in the presentation of puppet plays and dance-dramas based on the literature of the Mahabharata and Ramayana.

Among the many kinds of gamelons in Indonesia, one of the most famous is gamelon of Bali. Though all the instruments in a set are in the same scale, half are 'Female' instruments which are tuned slightly lower than their male companions. When the two groups are played together they create a shimmering throb because of the beats caused by their tuning difference and this lively sound is characteristic of Balinese ensembles.

Among the South East Asian instruments, we find the stringed instrument kudyapi of phillipines as a common instrument in Thai, Malaysia and Indonesia. Its ancestor is claimed to be the kachchapi Vina of Indian chordophone variety. It has many more South East Asian and South Asian relatives such as the three stringed crocodile zither of the more in Burma, the more abstractly shaped Thailand chakay zither the multi stringed sundanese Kachapi zither with movable bridges and the Borneo Kachapi, Kasapi or Sapeh which is a plucked lute with one to three strings.

Here it is important to be aware that a word is transferred from one concept or instrumental type to a very different form as it moves from culture to culture or even within one culture over a period of time. These are called floating terms and one cannot presume that the same term will mean the same thing when it is found in a new cultural context. when we look at the multiduous variety of musics, a fundamental question arises as to whether there are any universal principles in music? In a broad sense there does seem to be a basic need for musical tension and release with all their melodic or rhythmic implications (Malm).

Music is obviously as much a part of culture as a hoe or a potsherd. More than some aspects of culture, however, it has the abiliy to be emotionally moving and aesthetically pleasing. Every style of music contains an inner logic that can be understood and admired only if one is inclined to listen to it on its own terms. It is also true that every style of music is intercultural. With reference to the theatre, the intercultural concepts can be very well noticed in the Ramayana Theatres of South East Asia.

Ramayana Theatres of South East Asia and India

Though Malaysia is a federation of the different states, the earliest and the richest cultural legacy is from India. India's chief contribution to South East Asia and particularly to Malaysia are Religion and Arts especially dance and drama. The Indian influence of Indian culture is prominent in West Malaysia. The West Malaysia was formerly known as Malaya is the peninsula stretching from Thailand to singapore. The Northern states of Kelantan, kedah and Trengganu possess rich musical and theatrical traditions. Most of their indigenous music is associated with theatres and with ceremonial and ritual acts involving Hindu beliefs. The influence of Indian. Theatre is found especially in the north east in the state of Kelantan where many of the plots of the Wayang Kulit or the shadow puppet play are based on the stories of Ramayana and Mahabharatha and also the other traditional Theatres of Malaysia such as Ma'yong, and Bangswan which are influenced in their techniques of production by Indian traditional Theatres.

"... it should be noted that in South East Asia, theatres in which the shadow play exists have all at sometime in their history been under the influence of Indian culture. ... it is in India that we must seek the origin of shadow plays of South East Asia." (Amin Sweeney : 1972) The Malay Theatre Wayang shows many perceivable traces of Indian influences. There was a cultural interchange between India and Malaysia from very early times. The shadow and puppet theatres show the spread of the Indian Influence to the South East Asian countries in general with the Hindu rulers expansion of their territories with Indian Epics. The Chayanataka or the shadow play originated in India. They are mentioned in the epic Mahabharatha which dates back to 2nd century B.C. The Hanuman , Nataka Dutha Angada and Ramabhudaya are some of the famous shadow plays of India which deal with the stories of Ramayana.

The Ramayana had become the basic source for shadow plays from 15h century onwards in South East Asia when Hikayat Seri Rama was written. The shadow plays in Malaya have been popular not merely for their entertainment value but also for their spiritual content as one finds in India. The kudiyattam Bhgavata meal and Ramlila have spiritual value besides the entertainment purpose.

In Laos, Cambodia, hailand and in some parts of Malaysia the common term for dance is Ram, Rom or Lom which indicates the tremendous influence of Ramayana over these theatrical traditions.

Prof. Mazundar states The early products of art are distinctly Indian in conception, technique and execution and almost every phase of the medieval art of India is represented in Malaysia. Since the similarities are so striking, there is a lot of possibility that the theatrical traditions of Malaysia drew inspiration from India and that the cultural influences mught have started from the epic age and the process miht have developed through the centuries and might have reached the present state of development in their traditional theatres like Wayang Kulit, Ma'yong, Bangswan and others. The Indians who have settled in Malaysia associated themselves closely with the native population and the result was the fusion of the two cultures. The Indians were in contact with Malaya long time back and many of them have also became immigrants which paved the way for acculturation and fusion of Indian Traditional theatrical concepts in the shadow plays and also with their other traditional theatrical. The Malayan name for shadow play theatre is Wayang and they very much imitate the Chayanatakas or the shadow plays of India. Prof. Winternitiz holds the view that Mahanataka which is a shadow play has great resemblance in the Wayang plays. Mahanataka is one of the oldest sanskrit plays of Chayanataka type. In the traditional theatre of Orissa "Ravanachya" is an ancient shadow play. The puppets are made out of deer skin which factor is found in the wayang kulit of today in Indonesia and Malaya. The wayang is very much associated with religion and in India the shadow theatre forms have pronounced religious association. The Thol Pava Koothu which is the shadow theatre of Kerala retains its ritualistic character. The Tholu Bommalata of Andhra, Togalu Gombe atta Ravanachaya of Orissa which are the traditional folk theatres of India (shadow plays) have influenced the Wayang plays in Malaysia, greatly.

Wayang like the Indian folk plays is always performed in the open air and the play will go on throughout the night and will end in the early morning. It is performed in a thatched shed and one side will consist of white cloth behind which the Dalang or the puppeteer will manipulate the puppets which are made from deer skin (kulit) before a hanging lamp which throws the silhouettes upon the white screen as shadows.

The characters can be easily identified on the screen by their shape of the body. A profile with sharp nose and receding forehead in an unbroken line is immediately recognised as one of the Gods or Heroes; a figure with a snub nose and irregular features is a demon or evil spirit. For the entrace of each character, the orchestra will play the tune which will be followed by a song. This feature is found in all the traditional folk theatres of India where the character is introduced with a song. The songs known as Suluk which brings out the mood of the character resembles the sloka which are sung in the Ravanachya shadow play of Orissa. The tradition of the appearance of Vidushaka or Jester in the Indian folk plays can be found in the comic characters of the Malayan theatre Semar and Tuvas or Cheamuris. Wayang shows are very often performed before a large audience and they are staged on the festive occassions to ensure happiness and ward off evil. The Indian influence however is noticed not only in the stage version of the stories but also in the techniques of the whole presentation. The performances are preceeded by ritual offerings and invocations to Gods and Goddesses. This can be seen in every traditional folk theatre of India at the Puravaranga ceremony where the Rangapuja and invocation of Gods and Goddesses are performed before the actual play begins.

In Malaysia there are three types of Wayang which are known as Wayang jawa, Wayang Siam, and Wayang Gedak. All three are leather puppet shows and have the Indian cultural influence. The Malaysian Ramayana is found in two main traditions, the oral and the literary. The oral tradition is used by the players of the shadow puppets and the reciters of the tales. The standard shadowplay Wayang text is called Ceritra Maharajah Wana which means the Charithra or history of the

Maharajah Rawana. The shadow play of Orissa in India has the name Rawanachaya and the text is called the story of Rawana. The season for the wayang play is from the harvest season to the next rainy season. In India the Yakshaganas of Karnataka are performed only during the season. The wayang is performed on invitation by wealthy or at the religious function Bujama which relates to the spirits or Henyemah for warding off diseases and drought. This also reminds the Indian traditional theatre of Karnataka Yakshagana which are performed for the same purpose.

The Malay peninsula has the oldest form of theatrical entertainment known as Ma'yong. It is an ancient and primitive dramatic art which has been preserved almost intact through the ages. The Ma'yong is performed by a group of professional players who tour the country side giving performances in the houses of the local Chief's or Raja or for the village public for the rituals. The stage is set in a palm thatched shed enclosed on three sides where the performance will take place while the audience will be sitting or standing in the open air. There is no scenery and masks but the make-up and costume will help to identify the players. It includes stylised dances, solo choral singing and drama. The orchestra will consist of one Rebab, many drums and gongs, a native flute, castanets and staccato instruments with a wooden keyboard. In the village of Kelanton, this theatre is still popular and performed as part of the ritual, the healing Ceremony. The Pawang is the indispensable character in this play who is similar to the Sutradhara of the Indian traditional theatres. Before the actual play begins, there will be the worship of Lord Shiva at a preliminary function which is very much aking to the Indian culture of the traditional theatres, from the time of Bharatha who speaks about this ceremony in detail in his work Natyasastra, the treatise on dramaturgy, which dates back to 2nd cent A.D.

A purely modern form of entertainment which has become increasingly popular in recent years is Bangswan a musical comedy. It does not have much literary value but gives scope for the actors to improvise their dialogues. It resembles the traditional folk theatre of Tamilnadu which is known as Terukkoothu. In the "Oxford Companion of the Theatres" prof. Owen Rutter has remarked that the Play Bangswan came to Malaya from India. The Ramayana and Mahabharata stories are the main themes for folk theatres in many ways which indicates the intercultural aspects is Asian Theatres.

The Ramayana is an immortal epic, a "Mahakavya" in its true sense. Its greatness is indicated in the epic itself.

> "As long as the mountain ranges stand
> and rivers flow on Earth
> So long will this Ramayana
> Survive upon the lips of men"

The influence of the theme is reflected in various forms of the dance dramas and shadow plays in South East Asia. The story of the Rama seems to have bewitched and hypnotised generations of Asians belonging to countries with religious, literary and cultural traditions.

The Ramayana is performed in most countries having the Ramayana tradition. The performing tradition of the Ramayana has manifested itself in a great range and variety of forms having reional and stylistic variations from the dramatic recitation of the epic story with simple mime to the highly stylised and codified forms of dance and theatre and several forms of the puppet theatre - the processional and ritualistic "*Ramlila*" of North India and in the highly stylised and codified dance theatre "*Kathakali*" of Kerala ; in the highly theatrical "*Khon*" mask plays of Thailand and in the extremely lyrical dance drama of Bali and the "*Wayang Kulit*", the puppet theatre of Indonesia and Malaysia.

While the Ramayana theatre is an integral part of the colourful and multiform traditional theatre of Asia, it is distinguished by many technical features. It is the most representative and artistically rich sector of the traditional theatre often adding a new dimension to the epic story and giving new interpretations to the characters. The epic story with its legendary and mythical motives, eminently suits the stylised and convention-based traditional theatre of Asian countries.

In the Ramayana tradition, the idea of struggle between the forces of good and evil is so basic that it greatly influences the structure and nature of theatrical forms of various types. This idea of struggle is maintained and conveyed through a structuring of the form, peculiar to the Ramayana Theatre. The general pattern is that in the first stage there is confrontation between the two forces; in the second stage, challenge; in the third, conflict and combat; and in the fourth the victory of the good forces and defeat of the evil forces. This pattern is followed in a variety of forms of theatre dealing with the Ramayana theme. It is to highlight this idea of a spiritual conflict that in almost all the forms of the Ramayana Theatre, combat scenes dominate the performance, and are the most important and dramatic. In many cases, these are also most beautifully choreographed. The performers as well as the audience take great deliht in these scenes and get a kind of spiritual satisfaction in witnessing the defeat of the evil characters. In India, the burning of huge effigies of Ravana and his allies on the day of the enactment of the battles between Rama and Ravana is a grand ritualisation of this theme of the struggle between good and evil. In the '*Wayang Kulit*' of Indonesia, the Dalang introduces the principal characters and suggests the beginning of the plot, a fight between good and evil forces is the climax scene. At the end, good triumphs over evil.

The most ancient form of Theatre employing the Rama theme in many countries is the shadow theatre. It is the shadow theatre which has given rise to several forms of human theatre. the puppet theatre is also an oldest form using the Ramayana theme. Most of the Ramayana theatre influding pupet theatre evolved out of recitation which acts as baseline upon which the superstructure of the form is raised. In Indian strongest tradition of the shadow theatre is that of Andhra Pradesh, other regional traditions being those of Orissa, Karnataka, and Kerala. Notwithstanding many common features and conventions of figures and in the spokenword material and music content. Other forms of the puppet theatre. presenting Rama stories are the rod-puppets of West Bengal, the glove puppets of Kerala and the marionettes prevalent in Tamil Nadu and Karnataka. These Indian theatrical forms are spread out in many of the South east Asian Theatres on Ramayana.

The shadow theatre of Java and Bali are the most developed and highly cultivated theatres. With its deep ritualistic background and symbolic character, it has a great socio-cultural significance and truly mirrors the beliefs, attitude and traditions of the Indonesian people. With the spoken word material of rich poetic content; elaborate and codified music; magnificent and highly stylised figures; and the developed art of manipulation and vocalisation, Indonesian '*Wayang Kulit*' provide a total theatrical experience. There is a very strong Indian Influence in the Ramayana Theatre of Indonesia.

The tradition of the shadow theatre existed in Thailand which is "Nang Yai" a shadow play on Ramayana theme. The leather puppets are cut, embossed and painted elaborately. The movements of the puppets varied according to the characters. In the Cambodian shadow theatre, figures are projected on a large screen employing a number of puppetteers in a performance specially during the royal processions and war scenes.

Apart from shadow theatre, the Ramayana episodes are also presented in human theatre wherein actors participate with masks or mask like make-up. The "*khon*" plays of Thailand have similar triats of "*Kathakali*" of India. '*Khon*' means a mask. It is described as '*Masked Play*' or masked pantomime. It is the oldest theatrical form still seen in Thailand. In Kathakali, through the Masks are not used, the mask like makeup is done for the actors.

In Indonesia, Thailand and Cambodia, Rama is a hero but not a God. Often he is portrayed as a romantic hero, specially in versions where he sends out Sita in a fit of anger and envy after she had painted a portrait of Ravana on the fan. But in all versions, he is the embodiment of good. In all versions, Sita is associated with the Earth as to have come from the Earth and goes back to the Earth. Hanuman epitomises calm, solid loyalty. In all versions, he is connected with '*Vayu*' or wind and is the son of wind. In Indian versions, he is a bachelor but in Thai version, he is an amorous here, father of sons from Apsaras.

The Ramayana theatres is richest in episodes and spoken word material. There has always been a close link between the literary and the performing traditions of the Ramayana. Not only in human theatre, but also in the puppet theatre, the verses are taken from the Ramayana and other Rama poetry. It is this richness of literary content that has been the main factor for the sustenance and survival of the puppet theatre in Asia for nearly 2,000 Years.

During the medieval centuries, many poets wrote epic poems on the Rama saga keeping in view the performing tradition and its requirements. Some wrote the epic primarily to be performed. Thai Ramayana by King Rama IV and the Burmese Ramayana by Natak Kyaw Guang are dramatic versions of the epic story composed for theatrical performance. They are similar to Bengali Ramayana of Krittiwas and Vichitra Ramayana of Oriya which are used by the Ramayana theatres of these regions for textual material. The Ramacharitamanas of Tulsidas having a sound dramatic design, greatly enriched and sustained "*Ramlila*", the traditional theatre of North India, which deals exclusively with the Rama theme.

The Ramayana theatre is a theatre of stylisation and conventions, which are, in many forms, strictly codified. The stylised make-up and costumes, the codified gait and movements, the recitative chant like delivery of stylisation, the basis having been provided by a non-realistic, imaginative approach to the theatre. Stylisation is primarily concerned with the treatment of the actor's face, dramatic speech, movements and gestures. These factors are found in the Ramayana Theatres of South East Asia and India.

The highly stylised make-up in *Kathakali*, the powerful mask of *Khon* of Thailand and the lyrical masks

Balinese Ramayana Theatre

Balinese Ramayana Theatre

used in java are extremely effective devices to treat the actor's face. The stylised figures of the *Wayang Kulit*, the shadow play of Java succeed in creating a world of mystery and fantasy, deepening the meaning of the epic story. The masks and make-up of characters like Ravana, Hanuman and Jatayu have inspired craftsmen to evolve stylised approaches to their designs and varied interpretations of the characters. The embroidered Zarimask of Ravana used in the *Ramlila*, the life-size mask of Jatayu used in the *Ankia-Nat* of Assam, the mask of Ravana in the *Shahi Jatra* or Orissa and those used in Burmese dance-drama are most dramatic and powerful masks. The make-up and masks greatly accentuate and enrich the scheme of stylisation of the Ramayana Theatre, and impart to it a quality of other worldliness.

Along with the rich thematic and textual content, the Ramayana Theatre also has a rich and hihly developed music and dance content. Music is the very dynamics of this theatre, and it determines the pace, the rhythm and the movement of the drama. Specific melodies are fixed for various situations and actions to express different sentiments and moods to accompany the entries and exits of the characters. Orchestral pieces are often used as incidental music, specially during the fight scene. The orchestra plays in unison with the vocal line and repeats the melodic and enrich his gestures by an elaborate interpretation of the text. The theatrical presentation with rich music, striking poses and codified gestures builds up a spectacle of great choreographic beauty and pictorial charm.

The use of poetry, music, dance and mime, the intermingling of epic and lyric poetry and of narrative and dramatic material; highly stylised and choreographic style of acting illuminating the gestures, poses and movements of the actor; convention of speech, such as the alternation of prose and verse and a stylised, recitative and rhythmic mode of delivery; the use of singers and narrators; elaborate costumes, stylised facial make-up and fantastic masks and headgear with the concepts of colour symbolism and role division; freedom from the enities of time and placel elaborate preliminaries and rituals ar the main features which characterise the Ramayana Theatre of various countries. While the primary conventions and some of the practices have a Pan-Asian character, the secondary conventions and some of the practices are indigenous reflecting the values of the tradition theatre of the country concerned.

The similaities of elements, performing techniques and conventions between various forms of the Ramayana theatre in various Asian countries, indicate a two-fold process of transformation and of continuing mutual exchange. The whole pattern of migration, assimilation and continuing exchanges is complex because of two factors; one, the natural tendency and capacity of the indigenous artistic traditions to adapt and transform alien forms; and two, the coming of the influences from different parts of India and at different periods of History. The process of the transmission and transformation of the Ramayan tradition was never an one-way traffic. Some of the ancient Indian forms, performing techniques and conventions which disappeared from the country of their origin, still survive in certain South East Asian Countries, especially in Indonesia.

In the long tradition of the Ramayana Theatre, dance dramas with modern choreography evolved. The use and popularity of Ramayana episodes in the traditional dance "*Kechak*" of Bali, the dance-drama of Indonesia and of Thailand, Cambodia and Burma have been structured based on the shadow theatre. "*Kathakali*" in India represents a perfect integration of visual and aural effects in plastic form. "*Kathakali*" was first called "Ramanattam" (17th & 18th centuries) which later transformed into "*Attakatha*" and still later "*Lathakali*". Ramanttam was a series of 8 pieces covering the entire story of Lord Rama starting from *Putakameshti* sacrifice and ending with the fall of Ravana. It was in Malayalam and acclaimed as a great Art. Ramanattam players sang the padas and used masks. A change was introduced by Prince Vallathol Thampuran by providing separate singers and masks were replaced by make-up, mudras were accentuated; a variety of percussion instruments were used, costumes were worn and mime turned into mimicry. Thus *Kathakali* evolved as a word tone drama, a dumb show.

The Ramayana tradition in Indian and South East Asia, because of its pervasive character and deep-rootedness has greatly influenced the beliefs, customs and life styles of the people of these regions comprising of different ethnic and cultural groups. It has enriched the performing and visual Arts. Rama is an *Avatar* of Visnu in Hindu tradition, a Bodhisattva in Buddhist tradition, Shalaka Purush in Jain tradition and a believer of Islam in Muslim tradition. It is this cross cultural perspective of the Ramayana tradition which is its most fascinating and rewarding aspect and Ramayana Theatre is popular not only in India but throughout South East Asia - a fine example of Intercultural concept in Theatre.

CHAPTER VIII

INTERCULTURALISM IN THE NON-CLASSICAL MUSICS OF SOUTH ASIA

The subcontinent of South Asian comprises of the Countries India, Pakisthan, Bangaladesh, Srilanka, Nepal, Bhutan and Maldives. The South Asians are predominantly religious in their outlook. The religious orientation pervades in every sphere from social and economic life to literature, Arts Music and other performing Arts. the three major religions in South Asia are Hinduism, Buddhism and Islam. The meaning of the text and melody of the religions chants of the three religions overlap and a common thread runs in the tune of these religious chants and songs. The performance of these religious chants as well as the context by their performances have commonalities.

The people of the entire region of South Asian are unified by common cultural and ethical outlook. Music, dance, drama, ritual customs, modes of worship are similar throughout the sub-continent even though the regions have been divided into Kaleidoscopic political patterns through centuries. The religious music is cultivated in South Asia with the spirit of dedication an offering of the Almighty. the wide field or musical phenomenon in South Asia ranges from the relatively simple two or three tone melodies to the complicated Art music heard in concert halls. Among the non clasical musical forms the religious and folk musics are essential elements, in many of the activities of daily life and plays a prominent part in most of the social and religious rituals. Much of this music could be described as functional for it serves all utilitarian purpose. These songs are sung by all members participating in the activity and not sung for entertainment.

The cultural unity begins in the non-classical forms of South Asia and flourishes in the classical forms by the co-existence of the familiar Hindustani and Karnatak system of Music in India.

As Religion plays a very crucial role in the musical cultures in South Asian Countries, South Asia stands rather unique in the sense that the three great religions of the world - viz Hinduism Islam and Buddhism Co-exist not only with religious tolerance but also in giving respect for the other religious group. the religious pluralism of this region is so prominent at the national as well as regional level. When we look at the break down o the major religious communities in this South Asian Countries, it is interesting to find that the majority community in one nation becomes a distinct minority in the neighbouring country and vice-versa and this phenomenon brings forth the cultural unity in religion as well as in music.

Bangladesh

Bengali people and their poets have always glorified their country as the "land of music". Songs and music have been handed down through oral tradition and only the texts of the early Bengali songs have been written down. Vocal music dominated and the flute is often used as solo instrument. Bengali music is melodic music which is performed either solo or chorus and sometimes responsorial.

The earliest reference to Bengali music is found in the Charyagiti, a colection of songs which belong to 10th 12th Cent. A.D. Buddhist poetry were sung in rituals.

These poems, which are the earliest writing in Bengali use the term raga and name specific ragas such as Bhairavi, Gurjari, Bangala.

The introduction of the Vaishnav Cult of Hinduism into Bengal in the early 16th century brought forth the musical activity - kirtan or the Padavali Kirtan. The Vaishnava revival resulted in a rich outpouring of poetry which came to be known collectively as vaishnva padavali and also as Vaishnava giti. These songs are in praise of Krishna and developed into an elaborate musical tradition with a direct religious appeal.

The impact of Islamic religion on Bengali social and riligious life resulted in the introduction of new genra of songs dealing with Islamic religious traditions and legends. The sufi cult of Islam, coupled with Bhakthi Vaishnava devotion and Hindu-Boddhist Tantric philosophy and rituals prepared the ground in Bengal for the emergence of the important mystical sect, the Boul, drawn from both Hindu and Muslim communities.

During the late Mogul period secular songs and musical styles became popular in urban centres and the great demand for such music stimulated the creation of new song forms such as Tarja Kabigan, half-akharai and tappa. These forms are inspired by the Mushaira (public poetic competitions of Arabia) tradition which is popular among the Moslems of North India and Pakisthan. The Bengali Tappa differ from those of Punjab and Lucknow Tappa styles and are known as Nidhu - Babur Tappa.

Bengali gazals are very popular and they are akin to Urdu gazals on Islamic themes.

Rabindrasangeet is another widespread form which are on the model of drupads but with scope for western ornamentations and harmony.

Bhatiali songs are prevalent in the river areas of Eastern Bangladesh and known as boatman's songs which express philosophical ideas. They are metrically fluid, non-rhythmic and are sung in slow tempo. It is sung with the accompaniment of a drum or thin brass gong.

Mushidi and Marfati are the religious and devotional songs of Muslim Community. They are purely Islamic with themes in praise of Allah. Jarigan is another narrative song tradition of Muslim Community with religious or political themes in Bangladesh.

Among the musical instruments, some are indigenous while other are borrowed from Moslem cultures. The Banshi or the flutes of various types are indigenous. The Ektara or gopitantra of the Boul singers is different from the Ektar used in the other parts of India.

The Sarinda, a three stringed fiddle and the dotara, a four stringed plucked lute are important folk instruments in the rural areas of Bangladesh and these two instruments were imported at an early date following the advent of Islam.

Khol, the indispensable accompaniment for kirtan is an indigenous instrument. Manjira (small pair of brass bells) khanjari or Kar Tal (small pair of brass cymbals) and Kanshar (a small thin gong played with a stick) are idiophenes which are used in kirtan and Boul singing.

Thus we find the musics and musical instruments of both Islam and Hindu traditions surviving side by side and sometimes as an adaptation of either of these traditions is made which result in a form with mixed traditions such as Boul Sungs of Bengal in Bangladesh.

Srilanka

In Srilanka, the Major religion being Buddhims,

the Islam and Hindu, faiths are minorities, Music in Srilanka has always been associated with dance. The ancient Sinhalese Treatise "Sangeetha-Sasthra" defines music as a three fold art including Nacca (dance) gita (music) and Vadita (instrument). this work dates back to 2nd cent. The Ancient music literature of India also define Music or Sangitha as Geetam Vadyam Nrutyam Cha Sangithamuchyate which means that Gita (Music) Vadyam (Instrument) and Nrutya (dancer) together forms sangitha or Music. With the establishment of Theravada Buddhism in the 3rd cent B.C. & subsequent Buddhist centres of the educational system especially in Pirivena (monastically sponsored centres of higher education) music and drama were curtailed. The degree in which puritanical Buddhism was practiced however, varied with the religious disposition of the ruling king, patronage of the arts by the king and the aristocracy was common in having Vedda women dancers in Kandyan court. Kings of the later kandyan period were from South India and introduced carnatic musical instruments such as vina and mrudangam besides some of the folk dramas terukkuttu and the lyrics in the vannama and Viraha mustly love poems adopted by the Sinhalese about the 19th Cent. The parampara a school the taught religious rituals involving song and dance, primarily performed by men developed at the same time as the Pirivena; each parampara was different and keen competition between the different schools perpetuated highly developed forms of dance and drumming.

The original subjects of kandyan dance were the Hindu myths, particularly the crossing of Rama into Lanka, but gradually other legends were added to the repertory. Under the Kandyan kings the genra was admitted to the Buddhist temple and it is still performed in the month of August as part of the annual perahera festival during which the Buddha's tooth, enshrined in the temple of the tooth at Kandy is carried in a street procession escorted by costumed elephans, palanquins, drummers, singers, dancers and robed Buddhist monks. The Udakhi (hour-glass shaped drum) Talampota (a pair of hand cymbals) and Tammattama (double kettle drum) are the percussion instruments used often during rituals and one can find these instruments used in the temple rituals of South India.

In Srilanka, the influence of both North and South India has been considerable and is obvious in the sinhalese adaptation of Indian forms such as Nadagam (folk drama from South India and viraha (love songs). However Srilanka had traditional dramatic forms such as kilam (a masked folk drama with chanted poetry, dialogue song and dance) and sokari (a mimed story performed by masked dancers) before the introduction of Nadagam. The maddala (Drum) and the Tamil Isai were introduced to Srilanka along with Nadagam from South India.

During the first half of the 20th century Nurtiya, a North Indian theatre was introduced in Srilanka through the Elphinstone Theatre group. This genra related to the North Indian Ragadhari system of music which had new melodies and were rapidly accepted. Indian influence increased with the teaching of Hindustani classical music in Sinhalese schools and of Carnatic music in Tamil schools.

During the religious rituals, the drums and horns play an important role in the Buddhist cultural frame work which reminds the Indian influence where the horns and drums are used to bring the mystic effect in the religious rituals. For the Hindus, the dance and music are part of religious rituals and also believe that music and dance have divine origin. Sinhalese in Srilanka also believe that their music and dance in religious rituals of folk type are divine in origin. Their beliefs about the sounds of various folk musical instruments have much to do with Hindu mythology. For instance, they believe that the drum had its birth from the mouth of Brahma, timing from his teeth and songs from his tongue. The traditional artists believe that timing had its origin in the Dance of Shiva and Uma, According to tradition, the Sinhalese rhythm system consists of 216 fundamentals. The Rhythm consist of 32 Talams or rhythmic time measures 64 Soudam or varieties of drum beats in Salutation of Gods, 21 sural or elaborations, 27, Podi sural or rhythmic subdivisions, 15 vandamanam or narratives to be played and sung as offering to Buddha, 16 Dakum on drum beat pieces are played in the presence of God or the king in the form of salutations, 40 Adpadas or forty half heats are performed. The rules of drumming in both up country and now country sinhalese traditions were in Sanskrit originally which later changed to sinhalese language owing to oral transmission by non- literate artist.

The Hewisi drumming is also known as Sabdapooja or the offering of the Sounds to Buddha is a popular ritual. The main instruments used in Hewisi drumming are the Dawula or the cylindrical drum, Tammattama the double kettle drum and Haqranawa or the temple oboe and sometimes accompanied by Mangul bere or Gatabere the auspicious drum in the Kandyan tradition or the yakbere the devil drum in the low country tradition. Though this offering of sounds is made in the daily services of the Buddhist temples, a special place to witness this ritual would be the Temple of the sacred Tooth-Relic in Kandy (Dalada Maligawa). There one has the opportunity to listen to a variety of drum beats during the services customarily performing thrice a day; morning, midday and the evening. the drumming is also performed for anointing ceremony, drumming for the waving of the light and for Arti circle drumming (Alattipade)

These offerings of the sounds are found in various minor Buddhist temples. A special beat is played at Pirit chanting ceremonies or chanting of the sacred scriptures. During the ceremony of offering of meals to Gods, the Multan Mangalle which is a special kind of drum pattern is played.

Many traditional families of drummers can be found scattered over the central region of Srilanka. These family traditions or guruparampara are often referred to by their place names because they maintain distinct styles of playing. In Indian Music tradition, the gharanas or guruparampara is named after their places in the Hindustani Music tradition. Each guarana has a distinct style of its own.

When all the veteran gurus get together to perform the homage of the drums, there is a method by which they take the pride of place among them. For example, if the ritual is performed within the city of Kandy the chief drummers (Panikkyas) of the temple of the sacred Tooth-relic must be the leaders. This type of hierarchy is found also in the South Indian temple performers. The Nagaswaran performer attached to the temple takes the pide of place though he may be a mediocre player at the temple ritual when great Nagaswaram players from outside may be asked to participate in the ritual. Thus the cultural affinities of Hindustani and Karnatic traditions can be recognised in the performing traditions of music in Srilanka. The custom of paying homage to Gods and deities may have found its way into the Buddhist tradition through the influence of Hinduism. In Tiruchur, a place in Kerala in South India, the homage is paid through the drumming at the Pooram festival where more than one hundred drummers take part and exhibit their talents in the art of drumming and offer the drumming cultural exchange program of Government of Indian made me understand the Hindu and Buddhist traditions in the use of music and musical instruments in the religious music performed at the Srilankan Temples.

Nepal

Nepal is inhabitated by a large number of tribes, the two most important of which are Newas and Gurkha. Because of this phenomenon, variety of folk songs are found in abundance In the past, Buddhism was prevalent but through the centuries Hinduism became the dominant one. There is a genuine Hindu temple dedicated to Devi Sitla directly within the Monastery of Swayambunath the most sacred Buddhist shrine in Nepal, which is visited yearly in thousands of pilgrims of either faith. Nepal has a wealth of religious songs such as.

1. **Astute** - a Hindu prayer.
2. **Malshiri git** - a song (geet) which describes Durga's Victory over demons. It is sung during Durga Puja rituals. In a broader sense Malshiri git is applied to any Hindu religious song.
3. **Balum git** - sung only by men. The texts are from the Ramayana and Mahabharata.
4. **Boddheshela** is a Buddhist religious song.

   In the monastry of Swayambunath, Buddha is considered as a Hindu God and the songs are sung by Hindu priests as well as Buddhist monks.

Among the folk songs Rateli geet is a marriage song sung by the bridegroom party. Nani Phulaune geet is the cradle song. chaite geet is a song sung in spring. Bilap is lament song, Rasia geet the love songs of the peasants are very popular. These songs have enormous cultural and melodic similarities with the folk songs of North India.

Several song types have been imported and absorbed in the music of Nepal such as gazals, and Punjabi Heer songs from North India. The majority of songs of the Nepalese valley show characteristic features of Indian Music. It also has the similar melodic structure in the Antara or the second section of the song having the melody raising to the upper tetrachord like the songs of Indian Music (North and South). The complexity of melodic tunes and rhythm patterns very much have the affinity of Indian folk musics.

The drone instrument is provided with the accompanying instrument Sarangi, a stringed instrument with four strings. The wooden resonator is covered with hide and the top part is left open. The instrument is played on the open strings with a bow. It is closely related to the Sarangi of North India but different in its construction and playing technic. Similar, to Indian music tradition, this accompaniment provides the heterophony. During the religious processions, a pair of sohanai (shawn) is played. One plays the drone and the other plays the melody. A pair of Karni (long trumpets) narsingha (S shaped horns) Nagaras (pair of Kettledrume) Dholak (Two headed lacd drums) are used which bring out the Indo-Nepal cultural affinity in a marked way.

Bhutan

Though not much is known about the music traditions of Bhutan, the Buddhist Chants have the Tibetan and Indian influence and the musical instruments such as the Nagara, Naquarakhana, Sorna, Shanai and Narasingh are used in the Royal ceremonial music which is similar to Indian tradition. Most of the melodies are pentatonic and resemble the characteristics of Hindu Ragas.

Pakisthan

The Islamic republic Pakisthan's religious, art and

folk musics have links with the Hindu music of North Inda since it was party of India and acquired the political independence only in 1947. The folk songs including the life cycle songs resemble as the folk songs of Hindustan in its mode of presentation and function and the songs accompany a variety of traditional occupations. For example there are songs for grinding grains, spinning, making the children to sleep (Lullaby) for women and for men's work, songs for women for herdsmen, agricultural workers and drumming patterns for harvesting are found in Pakisthan which is very similar to India. some of these folk songs are commonly found and identical in North India.

Essentially all aspects of Indo Moslem culture represent a synthesis of varying proportions between foreign Moselem and indigenous Indian elements. The Indo-Moslem language Urdu developed as a result of the encounter of Persian, the court language of the early Moslem courts with the North Indian language Hindi and its dialects. The musical forms Gazal and Quawali in Bangladesh, India and Pakisthan have Urdu texts which are sung by Moslems and Non Moslems all over the subcontinent. During the Muharram, the Majlis which have the verses in urdu or the Farsi are performed by Moslems and constitutes a major part of the musical life of the Moslem community where secular Music making is generally discouraged.

The Majlis is one of the event where both professionals and amateurs perform in succession. The poems that are used in Majlis are religious poetry treating the subject of Husain's Martyrdom and the text for religious mourning. There would be no instrumental accompaniment for Majlis chant to have the clear articulation of the text. Majli hymns are strophic. The formal structure within the strophic is an adaptation of the standard pattern of North Indian classical song to the formal schemes of Urdu poetry. Majlis chant's music resemble the North Indian classical and light classical Modes/melodies. They resemble the Modes Kalyan, Bilawal, Khamaj, Kafi and Asaveri of Hindusthani Music.

Musical structure and idioms on the ritualistic (social & religious) music shows that they are generally monophonic with various types of accompaniments. Their primary dimension is the melodic line which may be performed as solo or by a group responsorially. Unaccompanied melody exists in life - cycle songs but most melody is performed with rhythmical accompaniments whether a simple pulse maintained by hand clapping or on idiophones, a complex metric pattern played on drums or both together. Instrumental drone accompaniment is usually found in addition to rhythmic accompaniment for these songs.

In Pakisthani Vocal Music, the textual structure is the basis for a variety of musical forms. Most songs consist of verses of two or four lines with varying rhythm patterns. The musical structure is strophic, and has the Sthayi Antara pattern of Hindustani Music (the North Indian Classical Music) Instrumental music based on vocal forms is generally governed by the same structure but may allow of embellishment, intermittent improvisation or alternative tune arrangement. Purely instrumental forms consist typically of a flexible series of short motive tunes, often symmetrical, built into rondo - like structure with intermitted return to one of the main tunes as one finds in the musical forms of India.

Music in life cycle ceremonies such as Birth, marriage and death are marked by special family gatherings. The women of the family together with female professionals sing a repertory of traditional songs specific to each occasion. Often these songs accompany a ceremonial activity. The songs consists of a variety of traditional songs and modern popular songs

The event culminates with group dancing. Men's gatherings include group singing and dancing as well as entertainment by professional folk musicians. By far the greatest number and variety of life - cycle songs are associated with marriage, the central life event in Pakisthan. Among these wedding songs, the pre wedding song for the occassion of engagement and mehendi and post wedding songs for wedding feast and later the dali (the bride's leave - taking from her family) are never missed and performed by family women old and young. They are very similar to Indian marriage ceremonies and their ceremonial songs. The professional musicians provide the instrumental music such as wedding band of wind instruments and drumming ensembles as one find in India.

The similarities in cultural behaviour can also be noticed with the other South Asian countries with the social ritualistic music of Pakisthan and India.

Harvest festivals and fairs, both religious and secular are occasions for all kinds of music making. Most popular throughout Pakisthan is a Circle dance accompanied by drumming and singing often interspersed with solo improvisations by trained dancers. In the fairs, musical plays puppet theaters solo singing and playing and group instrumental performances and singing and animal shows with musical accompaniment are provided. Among the musical instruments the Dholak or Dolki is the most widely used percussion instrument which is a double headed drum with a cylindrical wooden frame. The Dholki is used to accompany all types of singing including the whole genre of Dholak Git (Dalak songs). There are number of Dolki grat in Rajasthan in India.

The Damaru dugduggi is an hour-glass shaped drum played throughout Pakisthan by mendicants and wandering entertainers which is a common scene in India.

The duff a hand struck frame drum (wood or metal frame with brass discs inserted) accompany women's songs, throughout South Asia.

Naqqara, the clay or metal Kettledrums are played with beaters which are usually curved. The larger bheri and Noubat are played singly while Naqquara which are smaller are played in a pair. They are also found widely in Pakisthan, India and Bangladesh.

The principal idiophones are ghunguru and manjira (hand symbols) and chimta (metal tongs). the matka clay waterpot is used throughout Pakisthan as a flok instrument - where as Ghatam or Clay pot is performed as an accompaniment for South Indian classical Music concert. Among the Aerophones, the double reed Shahnai is associated with ceremonial out door music, which is identical with Indian tradition.

Punji is played by snake charmers in Pakisthan. The chang (patti) a Jew's harp is found all over Pakisthan and mainly by herdsmen. The Bansuri is another most common wind instrument all over the South Asian Region in Folk and Religious musics.

The sahnai is the instrument played through out North India for wedding and other ceremonies. Bansuri and Pungi are also popular instruments of North India with Folk music traditions. Pakistani folk music is melodic and includes a tonal center on the basis of which a great variety of scales can be identified ranging from three notes to over an octave. Most Pakistani folk music has some form of rhythmic accompaniment which sounds similar to North Indian Folk Songs.

The dominant tradition of sindhi music is the Rafi (wai) associated with Sind's most revered poet and mystic shaw Abdul Latif (1690 - 1752). Both his poems and their sur (melodic settings) which he composed represent a remarkable synthesis of Art and folk tradition. the poems express Islamic mysticism through the themes of Sindhi folk romances while their musical settings are based on melodic patterns derived from both classical raga and folk melody. Unlike raga, they are fixed by a pre-determined sequence of specific motifs. Within the kafi mode these motifs appear as a set of progression with measured rhythm as the principal melody. Between strophic poem, thematically related verses are inserted to a rhythmically free improvisation on the motifs and this part is called dohiro. Kafi music is performed all over the sind. In the villages it is sung in the form of mystic or solo love song to the accompaniment of yaktaro and the chapri or dandi both played by the male singer and sometimes accompanied by a drummer.

In Punjab most popular and versatile among improvising songs is the Mahiya (mahiyabalo, tappa) made up of the Punjabi verse form, the three tone tappa. Mahiya songs are sung at weddings or as leisure time entertainment often by compelling groups and they may deal with any kind of subject. Boli is (improvised couplets) the principal dance song for the men's Bangra and women's gidda dance. Similar motivic and tonal characteristics are found in many life cycle songs of Punjab.

Thc principal pathan singing tradition is closely linked with Pashtun poetry; its main locale is the men's gathering place, the Hujra. Hujra music is ideally performed by professional singers usually accompanied by rebab or sarinda and drum. The charbait one of the favourite song forms extols love or heroism in four line verses intoned alternately by two singers and sometimes repeated by all those present. The verses are interspersed with the freely intoned invocation ya qurban (oh my love) a typical musical formula of Pathan Singing. Which is Common in Pakisthan and India.

In Baluchisthan is than wandering professional performers are the principal music makers and the region is populated with hearding tribes. Liku (love songs) and Dastanagah (ballads) are the principle genre. These songs are most often accompanied on the saroz by the singer himself and consist of short verses sung in a rhythmically free style to one or two recurring melodic phrases which are often adapted for more than one song. The Saroz provides heterophonic accompaniment as well as an intermittent open - string drone, repeating freely elaborated versions of the melodic outline between verses.

Thus the intercultural concept in the non-classical music forms - the religious and folk music traditions of South Asia is prominent due to the overlapping of the religious concepts of Hinduism, Islam and Buddhism. Their influence is perceivable in the religious musics of the Pakisthan Srilanka and Nepal which represent the Islamic Buddhist and Hindu traditions and culture. The South East Asian music and theatrical traditions also reveal that intercultural concepts exist in their traditions from very early times through cultural contacts. One can very well understand that the Pan-Asian Cultural traits influence the Pan-Asian music cultures from the study of South East Asian and South Asian music and theatrical traditions.

The discipline Ethnomusicology which is a study of "Any" music with socio cultural perspective bringing out the Intercultural concepts in the world Musics. Since, the prefix "Ethno" before "Musicology" has lost its meaning it would be more appropriate to describe Ethnomusicology as "Intercultural Musicology".

CONCLUSION

What is ethnomusicology? It has been defined and answered in various ways by ethnomusicologists at different periods as the subject evolves during the period of time. Ethnomusicology preserved many exceptional, endangered music cultures from extinction Ethnomusicologists believe that one can understand music by understanding its extramusical causes. The extramusical causes are the society, the relation between culture and music Artists stimulate each other if the cultural environment permits the right kind of interaction. The influence on Music is of two types "operative influence" and "analytic influence". An operative influence changes the creation of music such as the influence of the cultural revolution on Chinese music or the Islamic influence on Hindu music which an analyst finds it convenient to construe.

John Blacking, one of the greatest ethnomusicologists says in his stimulating book How Musical is Man? that "Functional analyses of musical structure cannot be detatched from structural analyses of its social function. The function of tones in relation to each other cannot be explained adequately as part of a closed system without reference to the structures of the socio-cultural system of which the musical system is a part, and to the biological system to which all music makers belong. Ethnomusicology is not only an area study concerned with exotic music, nor a musicology of the ethnic – it is a discipline that holds out hope for a deeper understanding of all music. If some music can be analysed and understood as tonal expressions of human experience in the context of different kinds of social and cultural organization. I see no reason why all music should not be analysed in the same way" (Blacking 30-31, 1973).

My glimpse of the world of ethnomusicology has convinced me of the desirability of understanding music as an object in sociocultural domain as well as a musical domain, for purposes of musical adaptation and survival in our culture.

APPENDIX

Universals in Music

The Universality of the Pentatonic Scale

The scale "Mohanam" of South Indian classical music or Carnatic music is a pentatonic scale composed by whole steps and skipping a minor third in the keyboard instrument Piano where the notes of this scale can be performed on the black keys starting from F sharp. "Mohanam" is known as Boopãli of Bhoop in Hindusthani system (North Indian classical music) and in ancient **Tamil Music** literature, it is called *Mullaitheemapãni*. This scale can be described as a universal scale as the scale is found in every music culture in the world. It is widely used in the classical traditions in China, Japan, Korea, Thailand, Malaysia, Indonesia and in the Folk and Devotional music traditions of Tibet, Mangolia, Oceania, Africa, Russia and other Asian Countries, Australia, Europe and United States. Though the scale is present in almost every country, the Raga or Mode is presented in different styles as the construction of melodic phrases with the notes of the pentatonic scale vary and different types of ornaments are used for the notes for the different musical cultures in the world. This phenomenon reveals the Concept of Unity in Diversity in the World Music Cultures.

What is a scale? A scale is an abstraction, a collection of all the notes of a particular Mode or Raga which are arranged in the ascending and descending order in step wise manner. A Raga or mode consists of **melodic patterns** picking up the notes from its scale and presented with the ornaments of the particular musical culture. In Indian Music, the passing note or *Anya swara* of the Raga will be incorporated in the scale itself or will occur only in the *sancharas* or melodic patterns of the raga.

The pentatonic scale Mohanam consists of the notes *Chatusruthi Rishaba* (D), *Antara Gandhara* (E), *Panchama* (G), *Chatusruthi Dhaivata* (A) besides *Shadja* (C). This scale is described as a perfect scale as it contains the most consonant intervals, the Perfect V and Perfect IV.

[Sa-Pa, Ri Da DA GA]

[C-G D-A A - E] and

[Pa-Sa, Da-Rl, Ga-Da]

[G-C A-D E – A]

Because of this consonant intervalic structure, the scale of Mohanam is used in almost all the music cultures in the world and stands as an Universal scale. The scale Mohanam is transformed into Mohana Ragam in Carnatic music by the great composers through their compositions with various melodic patterns of ***sanchara's*** with different ornamentations on the notes. This raga Mohana is used in all the different types of musical compositions of Carnatic music such as *Geetham, Varnam, Keertanam, Kriti, padam, Jawali, Tillana, Daru* and even for *Mangalam*. An analysis of the various compositions in Mohana raga by various composers and different musical forms reveal that the melodic patterns or *sanchara's* of this raga are framed with *Janta Swara* (pair of notes) *Dhatu* swara (zigzag pattern) and *Jaru gamaka* (Portemento) besides the

Kampita gamaka (oscillation of the notes with its *anuswara* in medium tempo)

This Pentatonic scale gives forth different pentatonic scales fro *Ri, Ga Pa* and *Dha* through modal shift of tonic. The scales that derive through modal shift of tonic are the following:

Ri as Shadja or tonic	Madhayamavati
Ga as Shadja or tonic	Hindolam
Pa as Shadja or tonic	Suddha Saveri
Da as Shadja or tonic	Suddha Danyasi

The music of East Asia and South East Asia profusely use the pentatonic scale Mohanam and the other scales that derive from shifting the tonic on the other four notes *Ri, Ga, Pa* and *Da* of this scale. The scales are presented as modes in different countries using different types of melodic patterns and ornamentation on the notes, which gives forth the identiy of every music culture. There would be no *portamento* or *Jaru gamaka* and oscillation of the note in medium tempo touching the *anuswara* or *kampita gamaka*, which is found in the Carnatic music compositions, set in the Mohanam Scale. In other music cultures of Asia, the notes in the scale are performed as plain notes and sometimes with *vibrato*, the ornamentation of the notes are usually *Pdp*, *Dsd Srs* in the South East Asian Music Cultures. The range of this Mode or Raga is also limited to one octave or one octave and three notes at the most unlike one finds the range of the mode or Raga Mohanam in low, middle and Upper Octaves. For example, this pentatonic scale in China, Japan, Korea, Thailand, Malaysia and Indonesia where the scale is used in classical music traditions can be analysed.

The basic scale of China is the pentatonic scale *Wu Sheng* which is scale of Mohanam. The Chinese tonal system emerged as cyclin system. The Chinese Scale Wu Sheng emerged from a cycle of tones generated by blowing across the tops of a set of bamboo tubes closed at one end whose lengths were arranged in a set mathematical proportions. The acoustical basis for the method is the principle of overblown fifth. The Chinese arrived at 12 *Lu's* or pitches. The first five notes of the 12 *Lu's* became the basic pentatonic scale, which is called *Wu-Sheng*. This scale is equivalent to the scale of Mohanam. Interestingly, in ancient tamil music system, the Mohanam scale, which is called as Mullaitheempani, emerged from the cyclic system through the over blown fifth of the Bamboo flute.

The **Peking Opera** of China, which is an internationally well-known opera also abounds in the use of the Raga Mohanam.

The Japanese followed the Chinese music of 12 *Lu's*. Their music is characterised by five tone scales as well as seven notes scales. Their traditional theatres such as *Gagaku, Bugaku Noh* and *Bunraku* (puppet Theatre) use the music of sever-note scale but the rest of the classical music of Japan perform mainly the five notes scale. The two major pentatonic scales are *In* and *Yu*. The scale in resembles the scale of Mohanam and is played in *Koto*.. a plucked Zither of Japan with thirteen strings and movable bridge and six feet long.

The Korean Music also uses the pentatonic scale Mohanam profusely as it follows the ancient Chinese system of 12 *Lu's*. The pentatonic scale is called *Akshi-Jo*. This scale is played on *Kayakeum*, a plucked Zither of Korea (also played in Vietnam) with thirteen strings and movable bridges.

Thailand, Malaysia and Indonesia are the countries from South East Asia which use the pentatonic scale Mohanam profusely.

The tonal system of Thailand is also influenced by Chinese as the Thai people resided in China before migrating in the 13th Cent into the present day Thailand. They also have Indian influence as they have adopted the *Ramayana* Theatrical plays, which are dance dramas, and their music has many of the Indian scales. Among these scales, the scale of Mohanam is used in their Ramayana Theatres and *Mahori* Orchestra.

The Malaysian tonal system is influenced more by India and the pentatonic scales are profusely used more than the seven tone scales. The *Sapeh*, which is a plucked lute, is used as an accompaniment of *Kayan* dance where the songs in the scale of Mohanam are largely used. Malaysia also has the Indian influence on their theatre as they have the Ramayana theatres as dance dramas and puppet plays where in many of the Indian scales are used in their songs.

The tonal system of Indonesia uses both the seven tone scales as well as five-tone scales. Among the five-tone scales, the scale of Mohanam and its derivative scales from the modal shift of tonic are used mainly in their music. The five tone scale is called *slendero* and the seven tone scale is called *Pelog*. The Scale of Mohanam is similar to the *Slendaro Patet Nem* of Indonesian Music.

Besides the East Asian and South East Asian music cultures, the Hindusthani classical music tradition (North Indian Classical Music) calls the scale of Mohanam as *Bhoop* or *Bhoopali* and the scale is used in their different musical forms such as *Khyal, Dhrupad, Thumri, Tarana, Trivat* and *Bhajan*. The *Bhoop* raga uses the melodic patterns with move *Janta* swara (pairs of notes) and the *Meend* or *Jaru gamaka* (ornamentation).

The pentatonic scale Mohanam is found in almost every music culture in the world in their folk or classical tradition in the world in their folk or classical tradition which raises the fundamental question as to whether there are universal principles in music. In broadest terms, it seems that the Universality of Music is a phenomenon akin to the Universal belief on the presence of a Supreme Power or Almighty. God is perceived as the embodiment of sound and music plays a vital role in the religious rituals. The basic concepts of Music having seven notes, Twelve pitches, concept of consonance and dissonance are the same throughout the world music traditions. The concept of scale is also an universal one and there are many scales which are similar to Indian Music scales present in a few other music cultures of the world.

Among all these, the scale if Mohanam, a pentatonic scale with consonant intervalic structure stands as an Universal scale as this scale is present in every music tradition in the world in their classical or folk traditions.

Bibliography

Akin Euba, *Essays on Music in Africa, 2 Intercultural perspectives,* Elekoto Music Centre, Lagos & Bayreuth, African Studies, Bayreuth, Germany, 1989.

———, *Yoruba Drumming, The Dundun Tradition,* Bayreuth University, Germany, 1990.

Allen Warren Dwight, *Philosophies of Music History - A Study of General Histories of Music,* 1600 - 1960, Dover Publication Inc., New York, 1962.

Alan Merriam, *The Anthropology of Music* Northwestern University Press, 1971.

Amir Sweeney, *Malay Shadow Puppets* London, 1972.

———, *The Ramnayana and Malay shadow play,* Kulalampur, 1972.

Ashok Ranade, *Indology and Ethnomuricology, Contours of the Indo-British relationship*, Promilla and Company, New Delhi, India 1992.

Bruno Nettl, *Theory and Method in Ethnomusicology*, Mcmillan Company, London, 1964.

Boswell George W. and Reaver J. Russel, *Fundamentals of Folk literature*, Anthropological Publications, Netherlands, 1962.

Curt Sachs, *The Wellsprings of Music*, The Hague, Netherlands, 1962.

Charles Seeger, *Studies in Musicology,* University of California Press, USA, 1977.

Joseph Kerman, *Musicology,* (*Fontana Paperbacks and William Collins*), London, 1985.

David MCallester, "*The Astonished Muse*" Journal of the Society for Ethnomusicology, Vol. XXIII, (2) 1979.

Helen Myers, "*Ethnomusicology*" in Ethnomusicology an Introduction ed. by Helen Myers, The Norton and Grove Handbooks in Music, W.W. Norton and Company, London, 1992.

S.E. Bruno Nettl, *Theory and Method in Ethnomusicology* Mcmillan Company, London, 1964.

Boswell George W. and Reaver J. Russel, *Fundamentals of Folk literature* Anthropological publications, Netherlands, 1962.

David Rack, *Music of the Whole Earth*, Charles Scribner and sons, New York, USA, 1977.

Day, C.R., *The Music and Musical Instruments of Southern India* and the *Deccan*, B.R. Publishing House, New Delhi, Indian Reprint, 1974.

David Mcallester, *Readings in Ethnomusicology,* Johnson Preprint Corporation, New York, USA, 1971.

Durga, *S.A.K. Research Methodology for Music*, center for Ethnomusicology, Madras, 1991.

Discourse in Ethnomusicology, Essays in honor in George List eds. Card Caroline, Hasse, John Singer, Roberta L. Stone and M. Ruth, Ethnomusicology publications group, Indiana University, 1978.

Fox strangways, A.H., *The music of Hindoosthan*, Reprint, Oxford clarinden Press London, 1967.

Ethnomusicology an Introduction edited by Helen Myers, The North and Grove Handbooks in Music W.W. Norton and Company, London, 1992.

Explorations in Ethnomusicology Essays in honor of David Meallester ed by Charlotte J. Frishie, Detroit Monographs in Musicology, Number 9, 1986.

Gilbert Chase "*American Musicology and the social sciences*" in the Journal *Perspectives in Musicology*, New York, USA, 1972.

Harrison Frank, Hood Mantle and Palisca clauda, *Musicology*, Prentice Hali, New Jersey, USA 1963.

Kwabena NKe "*Integrating objectivity* and Experience in Ethnomusicological studies", The world of music, *Journal of the International Institute for Comparative Music Studies and Documentation,* Germans, 1986.

Joseph pacholezyk, "*Sufyana Kalam, The classical Music of Kashmir*" *Journal of the society for Asian Music*, Vol. X, New York, USA.

John Blacking *How Musical is Man*? University of Washington Press, Seatle, USA 1974.

Folk music and folk lore, An Anthology ed. by H. Biswas, Folk music and Folk lore Research Institute Calcutta, 1967.

Jaap Kunst, *Ethnomusicology* A study of its Nature, its problems, methods, 3rd Edition The Hague, Netherlands, 1974.

Mantle Hood, *The Ethnomusicologist* Mcgrawhill Book Company, New York, USA, 1972. Second Edition Kent State University. Kishibe Shigeo, Press USA, 1982.

The Traditional Music of Japan, ONGAKU NO TOME SHA Corporation, Tokyo, Japan 1984.

Merriam Alan, "*Comparative Musicology and Ethnomusicology A Historcal Theoritical perspective*" Journal of the society for Ethnomusicology, USA, Vol.XXI, 1977.

Nettl Bruno, *Ethnomusicology Definitions, Directions and Problems*, in "Musics of many cultures, An introduction" ed. by Elizebeth May, University of California Press, USA, 1980.

The European Airs of Muthuswami Dikshitar ed. by M.R. Sankaramoorthy Guruguha Gana Nilayam, Bangalore, India. 1990.

Sankar Sen Gupta and K.D. Upadhyaya, *Studies in Folk Culture*, Indian Folklore society, Indian Folklore Publication series, No. 6, Calcutta, 1964.

Tradition and its future in Music ed. by Tokumaro Yoshikiko, Report of SIMS, 1990, Mita Press, Osaka, Japan, 1991.

Intercultural Music, Vol. I, edited by Cynthia Tse Kimberlin and Akin Euba, Centre for Intercultural Music Arts, London and Bayreuth African studies series, Germany 1995.

Musics of Many cultures, An Introduction ed. by Elizebeth May, University of California Press, USA, 1980.

Michael Edward, *East - West Passage, The Travel of Ideas Arts and inventions between Asia and the Western World,* Toplinger publishing Company, New York, USA 1971.

Nazir A, Jairazbhoy, *The objective and subjective view in music transcription Journal for the society for Ethnomusicology* Vol. XXI, 1977.

Pragnanananda, Swami *Music of the Nations,* Munshiram Monoharlal, New Delhi, 1973.

Sourindra Mohan Tagore, *The Universal History of Music,* Calcutta 1896.

———, *Hindu Music from various authors,* 3rd edition, Chowkamba series, Varanasi, India, 1965.

Twenty six songs of Rabindranath Tagore ed by Arnold Bake Paris, 1935.

William P. Malm, *Music cultures of the Pacific, The Near East and Asia,* Prentice, Hall, New Jersey, USA 1977.

Willie Apel, Harvard Dictionary of Music, Second Edition, USA, 1978.

The New Grove Dictionary of Music and Musicians, Mcmillan Publishing Limited, London.

Reference : Journals

"Ethnomusicology", Society for Ethnomusicology, USA,

"World of Music" Journal of the International Institute for Comparative Music studies and Documentation, Germany

"Asian Music", Journal of the Society for Asian Music, USA.

Journal of the Indian Musicological Society, India.

"Perspectives in Music", USA.

Journal of the American Musicological Society, USA.

British Journal of Ethnomusicology, England.